IMAGES
of America

COLUMBIA

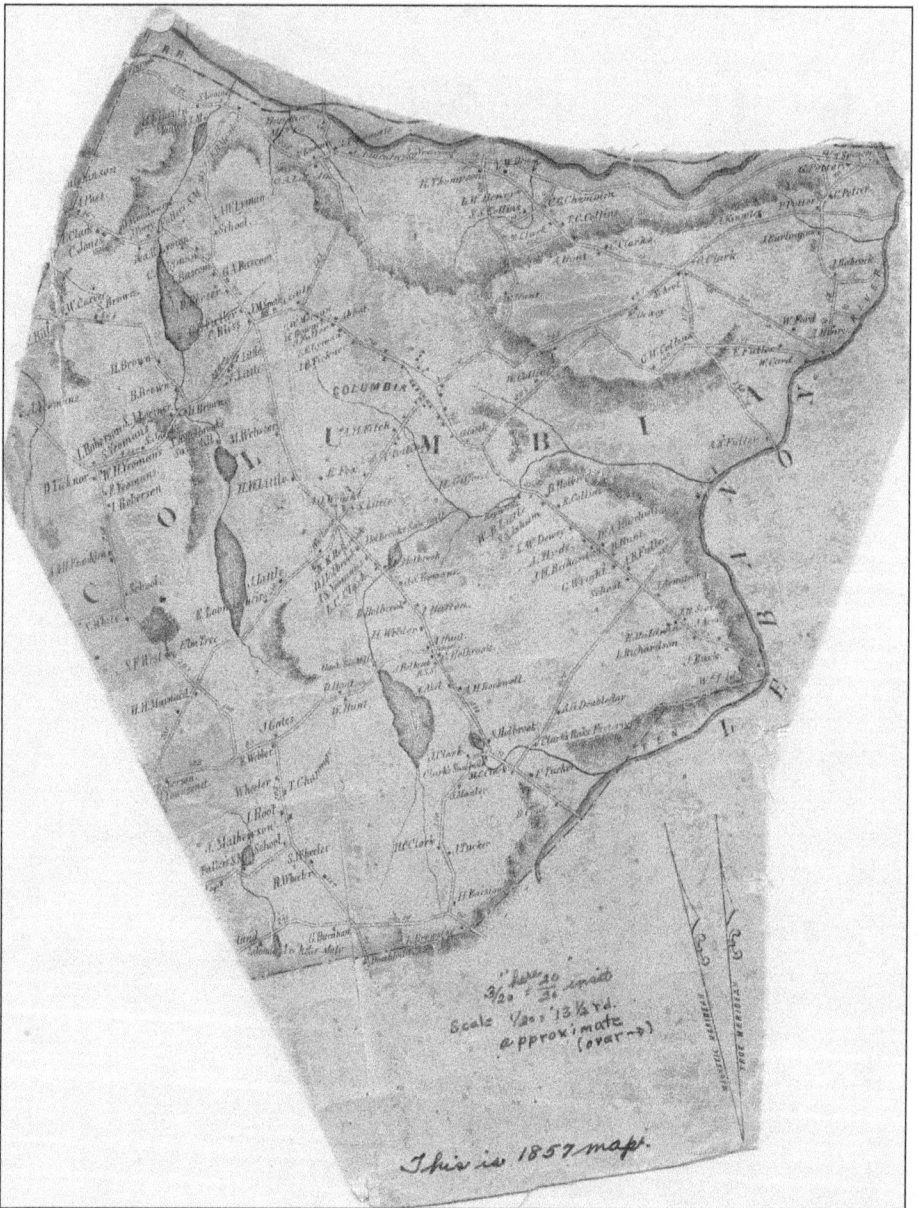

MAP OF COLUMBIA. This 1857 map of Columbia, from the *Atlas of Tolland County* published by Woodford and Bartlett of Philadelphia, shows topographic features, roads, mills, the Hop River Manufacturing Company, the New York & New England Railroad, property owners, and an elm tree on West Street that was 40 feet in circumference. Note the original pond and land area that was dammed in 1865 to create a reservoir, now Columbia Lake. (CHS.)

ON THE COVER: CAMP ASTO WAMAH. Virtues of patriotism, reverence, friendship, and loyalty were instilled in boys and girls at Connecticut's oldest continuously operating camp. Established by the Center Church of Hartford with the help of Columbia resident Evan Kullgren, Camp Asto Wamah, meaning "clear water," has been located on Columbia Lake since 1910. (Courtesy N. Mclean.)

IMAGES
of America

COLUMBIA

John Allen, De Ramm, and Ingrid Wood
for the Columbia Historical Society

ARCADIA
PUBLISHING

Copyright © 2013 by John Allen, De Ramm, and Ingrid Wood
    for the Columbia Historical Society Inc.
ISBN 978-1-5316-6610-1

Published by Arcadia Publishing
Charleston, South Carolina

Library of Congress Control Number: 2012942872

For all general information, please contact Arcadia Publishing:
Telephone 843-853-2070
Fax 843-853-0044
E-mail sales@arcadiapublishing.com
For customer service and orders:
Toll-Free 1-888-313-2665

Visit us on the Internet at www.arcadiapublishing.com

*To present and future generations of Columbia residents, that
they may continue to appreciate the history of our community.*

CONTENTS

ACKNOWLEDGMENTS

First and foremost, this book would not be possible without the encouragement and support provided by the directors of the Columbia Historical Society and the librarians of the Archives of the Saxton B. Little Free Library. We acknowledge prior publications and family histories of Columbia citizens and would like to thank teachers, librarians, and Grangers. We also thank The Women's Guild of the Congregational Church; Congregation Agudath Achim; Baptist Fellowship Church; St. Columba Roman Catholic Church; Camp Asto Wamah; Columbia Lake Association; town historian De Ramm; past town historians Adella Urban, Carmen Vance, and Gladys Rice Soracchi; Columbia Historical Society's Belle Robinson; Arlene Gray; Al Gray; Noreen Steele; Pat Grabel; Andrea Stannard; Meredith Petersons; archivist extraordinaire Joan Hill; librarian Su Epstein and her staff; Columbia Volunteer Fire Department; retired farmers and town officials; and Columbia Crossroads writers, artists, and naturalists who have already contributed to Columbia's rich history. This volume was conceived, in part, as a tribute to prior history keepers, complementary to their publications, and primarily as a photographic record containing as many objects as our editors would allow. We are mindful that, while photography emerged just before the Civil War, Columbia and Lebanon Crank date to 1699. This volume concentrates on a Columbia revealed in photographic images starting in 1880.

Thanks and appreciation for special contributions are due to June Squier, Nancy Nuhfer, Joan Hill, Tip Garritt, and Mike Morrill, who walked the Utley Hill mill sites; Nancy Mclean, director of Camp Asto Wamah; Laura Smith, curator of the Business, Railroad, and Labor Collections, University of Connecticut Libraries; Barbara Tucker, J. Eugene Smith Library, Eastern Connecticut State University; Carol Kubala, Saxton B. Little Free Library; Donna Baron, Lebanon Historical Society; and our editors at Arcadia Publishing, Lissie Cain and Rebekah Collinsworth.

The authors divided the tasks by chapter, with historian De Ramm collaborating and contributing numerous photographs and material throughout. Ingrid Wood wrote the introduction and chapters one through three, on Columbia's early history; De Ramm wrote chapter four, on Columbia's early institutions, the schools and churches; and John Allen wrote chapters five through nine, on Columbia Lake, neighborhood personalities, government, Columbia during wartime, and social and civic organizations up until 1970. We are grateful to Belle Robinson for reviewing the manuscript and providing insightful suggestions.

Photographs and postcards that are privately owned are credited to the name of the contributor. Courtesy credits are abbreviated as follows: Columbia Historical Society (CHS); Archives of the Saxton B. Little Free Library (ASBLFL); Archives and Special Collections, University of Connecticut Libraries (UCONN); and Eastern Connecticut State University's J. Eugene Smith Library Special Collections and Archives (ECSU).

INTRODUCTION

In 1804, "Columbia" was selected as the poetic and aspirational name for a northeast Connecticut township of 834 people whose families had already embraced the 22-square-mile highland frontier for over a century. The Massachusetts Bay settlers of the 1699 proprietorship established by Josiah Dewey, William Clarke, and Thomas Buckingham had kept their covenant with God and with each other. The first community was called Lebanon's Second Ecclesiastical Society, Lebanon's North Parish, or the familiar Lebanon Crank, after a sharp turn in the road from the center of Lebanon. It petitioned for independence in 1716, but was denied. Of Congregational faith and governance, the tiny parish was permitted to build two successively larger meetinghouses (the second painted sky blue), partly in response to Eleazar Wheelock's preaching a religious revival called the First Great Awakening. He was allowed to host a preparatory school in 1735 that later brought international and colonial acclaim as Moor's Indian Charity School. Lebanon Crank was able to establish five public school districts in 1773, and was allowed to create an extraordinary little colonial library, called the "Propriatory Library of Lebanon Crank," for public use by 1797. A high premium was placed on education and learning, oratory, music, poetry, reasoning, and the practical arts of husbandry.

As early as 1770, the first out-migration had begun in search of more land and opportunity. Tillable lands were spoken for, and the only remaining first-growth forested parcel was 1,000 acres known as Wells Woods. Prior to the American Revolution, Columbia's sons had already served in four colonial conflicts between 1701 and 1763. Families moved to Nova Scotia, the Wyoming Valley of Pennsylvania, or the safe frontier of central New Hampshire and Vermont to avoid the prospect of a bloody civil war with Britain. Those who stayed served in Lebanon's Sons of Liberty and a local militia called Lebanon's Second Troop of Horse. Lebanon Crank's Capt. Seth Wright and his troops were called up to fight in the battles of Lexington and Concord, then Bunker Hill, Harlem Heights, and Long Island. Not all returned, but 21 Revolutionary War patriots are buried in local cemeteries. On September 6, 1781, Rev. Thomas Brockway, who succeeded Eleazar Wheelock, put down his sermon and called all able-bodied men and boys of the parish to arms against the British for the burning of New London. Such was his passion that Brockway is said to have given £15 of his £90 annual salary to "the colonial cause until the enemy withdrew, and ten pounds a year until the Continental debt was paid." Mrs. Brockway conducted prohibited weaving and sewing bees. Innkeepers ministered to the sick and wounded.

Lebanon Crank was a colonial crossroads used by Gen. George Washington en route to the strategically important Trumbull War Office, the center for logistics, planning, and procurement. Approximately 5,000 French troops under General Comte de Rochambeau and 3,000 Continentals under General Washington used these crossroads during several military campaigns from October 1776 to November 1782. The French distributed an estimated 20,000 rifles, bayonets, and gunpowder; surprisingly, such bayonets still show up now and again. As Saxton B. Little stated in 1903, Columbia was entitled to its share of honors showered upon Lebanon for its contribution to the American Revolution.

The hilly terrain and plentiful water sources were conducive to early milling industries. Among the sources of water were the Hop River, Willimantic River, Ten Mile River, Dam Brook, the Utley Hill stream (now called Columbia Lake Brook), Gifford's Brook, Macht Brook, Clark's Brook, Mint Brook, Mono Pond, the dammed pond that became Columbia Lake, the Utley Hill upland swamp, and numerous vernal streams and watercourses. Recent archaeological surveys performed in connection with the Algonquin Gas Transmission pipeline construction revealed prehistoric quartz Stark projectile points near such water sources, suggesting the presence of a hunting and gathering society from the Middle Archaic period (8,000–6,000 B.C.). In the 18th and 19th centuries, Columbia inhabitants milled comestibles such as corn, rye, sorghum, buckwheat, and cider, and produced cotton warps, threads, yarns, silk threads, homespun, paper, papier-mâché, lumber, spindles, baseball bats, and fulled wool fabric for hats. Successful businesses scaled up to relocate to nearby Willimantic and Manchester. The Hop River Village claims the first large-scale industrial cotton mill in Connecticut, in 1837. The village was large enough to require its own school, built by William Jillson in 1885. Woolen plantation hats were manufactured at eight smaller mill sites located in each of Columbia's seven districts. Hat fabrication involved both a carding mill and a fulling mill. These hats were sent to the South before the Civil War. Fancy hats were shipped to New York City markets.

Columbia Reservoir was dammed by the American Linen Company in 1865, answering the need for a reliable and constant water level for the early water-powered textile mills in Willimantic. As steam and electric technology became prevalent, the reservoir was no longer needed to power industry and was sold to the Town of Columbia in 1933. The reservoir evolved into Columbia Lake, the site of summer cottages as early as the 1890s, Camp Asto Wamah in 1910, and the first public beach, near Brown's orchard, in 1915. The Columbia Lake Association was organized in 1935 to protect and oversee the lake as a community resource. Columbia Lake is today a private residential neighborhood.

Columbia's agricultural roots reemerged in the late 1890s. Columbia Grange No. 131 became the predominant social and cultural force, without the political overtones seen in Midwest rural districts. By 1885, two railroads crossed Columbia. In their wake, two stations were built, followed by a roundhouse turntable called Columbia Junction in nearby Willimantic. Dairy and fruit and, later, poultry products were shipped to large urban markets. Telephone and telegraph services were established by 1891. The "Four Corners" crossroads at Routes 66 and 87 was paved in the 1920s and then widened in the mid-1930s. Electricity came to Columbia in 1925. The first automobile repair shop appeared in 1907; by 1925, the personal automobile had replaced the horse-drawn carriage. Access to Connecticut's big cities by personal automobile for daily work was Columbia's first major step to exurbia.

Economic transitions following World War II, the Korean conflict, and the Vietnam War recast this once-remote rural town into a growing suburban residential and recreational community. Better state highway connections to Willimantic, Norwich, Manchester, Hartford, Providence, Boston, and New York were established. Columbia's section of The Hop River Corridor on Routes 6 and 66 is the closest equivalent to a commercial district, anchored by Columbia Manufacturing Inc. and several large automotive and motorsports sales and service dealerships.

Vestiges of Columbia's religious, revolutionary, and industrial past can still be seen at Potter Meadow; in the structures and cemeteries of Columbia Green Historic District; Utley Hill Preserve; Hop River Rail Trail; Airline (Rail) Trail; the 18th-century homesteads on Routes 66 and 87, West Street, Pine Street, and Cards Mill Road; the new park at Wells Woods; the Columbia Historical Society's collections; and the Archives of the Saxton B. Little Free Library. Of interest now, however, is the steady march of 21st-century progress and the tension between the desire for growth and commercial development on the one hand, and, on the other, the preservation of old-fashioned ideals of small-town residential and recreational well being.

One

Ye Crank in the 18th Century and Historic Columbia Green

In 1670, following King Philip's War, Lebanon Crank, now Columbia, was disputed Nipmuck territory that came under the authority of Mohegan Sachem Uncas and his sons Oweneco and Attawanhood (Christianized as "Joshua"). Upon his death in 1676, Joshua conveyed 1,500 acres of land to his friend Rev. Thomas Buckingham of Saybrook, Connecticut, and his children, as these were prime farming, hunting, and fishing areas along the Hop and Willimantic Rivers. Reverend Buckingham's sons farmed the area, but later records show grandson Capt. Samuel Buckingham built a "mansion house" in 1702 on Cards Mill Road. With a deed from Joshua's son Abimeleck, Reverend Buckingham sold these lands in 1699 to Sgt. Josiah Dewey and Capt. William Clarke of Northampton, Massachusetts, who, as original proprietors, in turn conveyed 20-acre lots to Massachusetts Bay colonists seeking refuge from Indian raids in the Connecticut River Valley. The colonists established a thoroughfare, now Route 87, and erected the Lyman sawmill near the Ravine and the Dewey gristmill along the Ten Mile River. These close-knit families petitioned Connecticut's General Assembly to become a township, which was denied. The settlement, called Lebanon Crank, or Lebanon's North Parish, was nonetheless allowed to have its successive meetinghouses and remained a separate parish until 1804, when it was incorporated and renamed Columbia. Lebanon Crank was a self-sufficient agricultural community in the crossroads of the Connecticut colony's northeast highlands. In 1735, Pastor Eleazar Wheelock established a preparatory school for young boys entering Yale and Harvard. In 1743, a Mohegan youth, Samson Occom, was allowed to enroll to learn English ways, and was so successful that local farmer Joshua Moor of Mansfield, Connecticut, donated funds to establish a charity school for Native Americans in 1754. Moor's Indian Charity School opened the following year. During the American Revolution, Lebanon Crank became a center for Lebanon's Sons of Liberty, led by Capt. Seth Wright. In 1769, he helped Wheelock move his school to the safe frontier in Hanover, New Hampshire. Lebanon Crank's activities supported the Trumbull War Office in revolutionary Lebanon.

WHEELOCK MEMORIAL, COLUMBIA. Erected in 1949 by the Connecticut Society of the Colonial Dames of America, this memorial includes the following inscription: "In 1755 Eleazar Wheelock, DD, minister at Lebanon Crank (now Columbia) founded near this spot Moor's Indian Charity School. In 1769 the school was removed to Hanover, New Hampshire. From this beginning arose Dartmouth College, Eleazar Wheelock, president 1769–1779." (Courtesy I. Wood; CHS.)

HOME OF ELEAZER WHEELOCK, C. 1910. The Wheelock House, built around 1735, was the original site of a preparatory school on 25 acres adjacent to the town green. The school emphasized training of young Native Americans in the rudiments of secular and religious education and in husbandry. The focus was expanded to include missionary work as well as the education of young women in the arts of housewifery. (CHS.)

MOOR'S INDIAN CHARITY SCHOOL BUILDING. This post-and-beam, clapboard building, built around 1755, has a vaulted ceiling and Franklin-type stove. Wheelock received solicitations to move his school to other colonies. This building later housed the Center School, one of the parish's original five school districts, established in 1773. The Center School, a one-room schoolhouse, remained in use until 1956. (CHS.)

WHEELOCK MIGRATION TO HANOVER. This interpretive mural was designed in 1950 by sculptor and artist Nelly Sweet Tuttle. The entire mural, a detail of which is seen here, shows the Indian School, an ox cart, a barrel of rum, a cow, Mrs. Wheelock beside her coach, servants, Indians, and a man on horseback, all headed toward a log house in New Hampshire. Wheelock stands preaching. Samson Occom is receiving money bags from the Earl of Dartmouth. (CHS.)

REV. SAMSON OCCOM. Among Wheelock's famous students, Samson Occom (1723–1792), a Mohegan, became a schoolmaster and Presbyterian minister. He served the Native American communities in Montauk, Long Island, and Mohegan, Connecticut, and founded a Christian community in 1785 in Oneida, New York, called Brothertown. In 1766, he and Rev. Nathaniel Whitaker of Norwich embarked on a two-year fundraising mission in Europe for the school, raising an estimated £10,000. This would have been equivalent to approximately $1.7 million in 2010 dollars. (CHS.)

SETH WRIGHT, CAPTAIN, 2ND TROOP
OF HORSE. An active militia leader
in Lebanon's Council of Safety
and the Sons of Liberty during the
Revolution, Wright (1726–1775) served
as longtime friend, confidant, and
financial agent for Eleazar Wheelock.
He funneled money and supplies to
Hanover, New Hampshire, during
the Coercive Acts (1773–1774),
when Boston was under siege and
Wheelock's funds from European
benefactors were cut off. (CHS.)

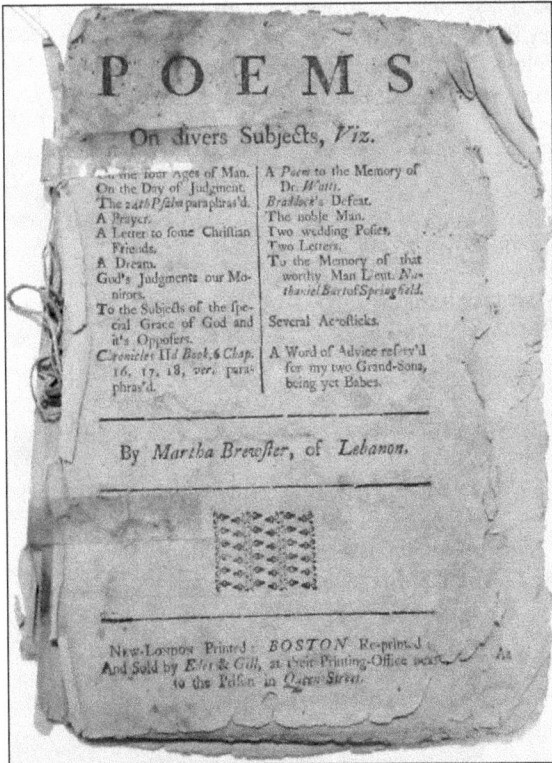

POEMS ON DIVERSE SUBJECTS, 1757.
Martha Brewster (1710–1757) was
influenced by Wheelock's sermons
on God's purposeful mission in the
New England wilderness. She wrote
on topics that defined the colonial
experience: preparations for military
invasions on the frontier, ravages
of war on surviving families, and
religious and ethical schisms within
The Great Awakening movement.
(Courtesy Lebanon Historical Society.)

POEM PRESENTED TO ELEAZAR WHEELOCK. This congratulatory note and poem was sent to Reverend Wheelock and his new bride, Mary Brimsmaid, who were married November 24, 1747. Mary Brimsmaid Wheelock, Reverend Wheelock's second wife, is depicted in this mural showing the 1769 Wheelock family migration to Hanover, New Hampshire. (ASBLFL and CHS.)

Lebanon December 4th, Anno Domini, 1747
Reverend, and Honoured, Sir,

Trusting your Clemency will Pardon what's Amiss,
And accept of a sincere Wish; I venture to present
The inclosed Lines, tho' Rude, and Undigested, they being
Only a faint Lineament of her Heart, who is with all dutiful
Respects and Affection,

Your's, Martha Brewster

ALL sweet Fruition now Betide,
The Venerable Groom and Bride,
Fresh Olives by a noble Vine,
May bless the World, for future Time,
And may the King of Glory Grace,
These Nuptials with Celestial Rays,
Of Joy, and Happiness Sublime,
Converting Water into Wine.

Your mutual Loves let still Increase,
And we be Blest with Truth and Peace,
Still Guide us as you've ever done,
And late Receive a Glorious Crown.
Seraphic Love your Hearts Inspire;
In comfort joyn the Heavenly Choir.
The fairer Palm, the higher Crown,
The lower will ye—cast it down.

Old Yard Burying Ground. A final resting place for patriots of four colonial conflicts and for parish families, this one-acre cemetery was deeded to the town by Eleazar Wheelock in 1760. Noteworthy are the gravestone carvings and witty epitaphs. Lebanon Crank favored local eastern Connecticut Puritan carvers Benjamin Collins (1691–1759) and his son Zerubbabel Collins (1733–1797), Obadiah Wheeler (1673–1749), and the Crank's own carpenter-turned-stone-carver, Jonathan Loomis (1722–1785). The stone of Lydia Bennitt, who died in 1791, includes its $7 price. It was carved by Zerubbabel Collins, who later moved to Vermont. It reads:

IN MEMORY OF
Mrs. Lydia Bennitt, the wife
Of Mr. Henchman Bennitt:
Who died March 31, 1791, in
The 46th year of her age.
All you that read with little care,
Who walk away and leave me here;
Should not forget that you must die;
And be Intombed as well as I.
Pr. 7 Dollars.

(Courtesy CHS, J. Hill.)

MILESTONE, C. 1763. Benjamin Franklin, joint deputy postmaster general, surveyed New England's post roads in 1753 and 1763. The later survey involved the use of the newly invented odometer, which, by counting 400 rotations of a wagon wheel, measured one mile. Milestones were maintained by local towns, as mandated by the Connecticut General Assembly. The Middle Post Road went through Lebanon Crank for a time. This milestone reads "18M NTH," indicating that it is 18 miles to Norwich Town Hall. (CHS.)

NORWICH TO HARTFORD STAGE, C. 1850. This postcard depicts the arrival of the Norwich to Hartford mail at the Hebron post office. Stagecoach mail delivery was instituted in the late 18th and early 19th centuries as postal routes evolved in the new nation. Rail coaches delivered mail to Hop River Station and Chestnut Hill Station in the late 19th century. (CHS.)

THE LANDMARK. At the crossroads of present-day Routes 66 and 87, this old inn, built around 1740, was used by French soldiers in 1780–1782 en route to Lauzun's encampment in Lebanon. The inn served as a stagecoach stop between Norwich and Hartford, and the *porte cochere* is still visible today. Formerly known as the Lebanon Crank Inn, the site was used as a farm and private residence until 1963. (CHS.)

WASHINGTON-ROCHAMBEAU REVOLUTIONARY ROUTE. Designated a National Historic Trail by Congress in 2009, the 680-mile route traveled by General Rochambeau in June 1781 follows a few miles of rugged roads and hilly terrain through Columbia. Four French regiments of 5,000 men and 3,000 American Continentals marched through Lebanon Crank during several military campaigns. (Courtesy DECD-CT.)

COLUMBIA GREEN, LOOKING NORTH, C. 1909. The National Register of Historic Places cites Columbia Green Historic District as an 18th- and 19th-century historic site due to its architectural unity, early religious and educational influence, and early industrial and commercial importance. A total of 42 major buildings, 32 associated buildings, 2 sites, and 4 objects make up this 35-acre district at the confluence of two colonial roads. This district, surrounding the original green, is

remarkable for the preservation and integrity of New England village structures built between 1740 and 1930. A walk around the green, extending one mile along Route 87, reveals building styles ranging from vernacular Gambrel, early Cape, Federal, Greek Revival, Queen Anne, Italianate, Gothic Revival, Bungalow, and Colonial Revival. No two structures are alike. (Courtesy National Park Service; I. Wood.)

COLUMBIA GREEN, LOOKING SOUTH, C. 1910. Elm trees planted in 1852 frame the landscape on the elongated green. Baseball, Columbia's favorite pastime, was enjoyed by spectators seated on the grass. The Congregational Church, administrative town offices, Yeomans Hall, Center School, a succession of libraries, post offices, general stores, and early inns defined the village center in the 19th and early 20th centuries. Social institutions such as the Masonic Fraternal Organization,

Grange No. 131, lyceums, and singing schools conducted their meetings in the Town House, the ballroom at the Old Inn, and later at Yeomans Hall. The roads were unpaved, but a new rotary is in evidence at the corner of present-day Routes 66 and 87. Missing is a Spanish Revival gas station, now the Collins Garage, not built until 1935, and a neo-Victorian gazebo, erected in 1980 by the Lions Club. (Courtesy I. Wood.)

ROTARY AT "FOUR CORNERS," C. 1909. This is a panoramic view of the new rotary with signage at the junction of what is now Routes 66 and 87. St. Columba Roman Catholic Chapel, originally a private home, built in the Greek Revival style, is hidden beneath the trees. All of the original structures near the four corners were demolished or moved to accommodate wider state highways in the mid-1930s. (CHS.)

ROTARY AT "FOUR CORNERS," C. 1932. This is a view of the rotary facing Porter's first store and post office, looking north from The Landmark toward former Route 6A, now Route 66 North. Columbia was electrified in 1925. The roadways were paved in the 1920s. The Porter Store building (left of center) was removed to another location in the 1930s. (CHS.)

Two

The Bounty of the Land

Columbia's hilly terrain, loam-type soils, small streams, ponds, and rivers made it suitable for pasture. Settlers in the 18th century recreated English farmsteads, with features such as cottage gardens, protective thickets of lilac, and segregated farm outbuildings. The four-part field system, an established practice throughout New England by 1790, revitalized nutrient-depleted soils cleared of first-growth forests for nearly a century. Seasonal weather patterns dictated mixed farming and home industry: planting, haying, and harvesting from April to October; and lumbering, maple sap gathering, tool-making, and produce processing from November to March. Subsistence agriculture was supplemented by beef-cattle ranching as Lebanon became a prominent stock center before the American Revolution. Cattle were walked to Boston and Norwich. Beef, pork, and other products were brined, barreled, and exported to England and the Caribbean by enterprising traders such as the Trumbull family in Lebanon. Ranching persisted into the early 1800s. By 1850, dairy cattle replaced beef cattle as productive breeds of milk cows were introduced. The emphasis on "export" dairy production focused on butter and cheese, then evolved to milk products as precursors to refrigeration were developed.

Two railroad lines, two depots, and a roundhouse turntable in nearby Willimantic served Columbia from 1840 to 1940, enabling rapid transport of perishable products to urban markets. Large-scale production developed with improved mechanization. The availability of block ice from Columbia's numerous ponds preserved dairy products and fruit, mainly apples and pears, during the early days of rail transport prior to refrigeration. Retiring Yankee dairy farmers sold their land to a new wave of immigrants from Eastern Europe in the early 1900s. Many started out in New York City, but a number of enterprising families settled in Columbia, seeking a less urban environment. They engaged in large-scale poultry farming. Today, Columbia's varied agricultural interests are much smaller in scale, but include diverse products such as hay, specialty game poultry, eggs, apples, pears, peaches, berries, tomatoes, cucumbers, squash, pumpkins, herbs, wine, llama wool, dairy cattle products, beef, lamb, pork, goat products, honey, maple syrup, timber, organic Christmas trees, and horse training and boarding.

BAILEY HOUSE. The pattern of 18th-century homesteads and farmsteads is still in evidence along major ridgelines, Routes 66 and 87, West Street, Lake Road, Pine Street, Cherry Valley, and Old Willimantic Road. The 25 remaining pre-Revolutionary houses and barns are testimony to an agrarian subsistence economy. The Bailey House, built around 1701, is an early farmstead located on West Street near Basket Shop Road. (CHS.)

STONE ENCLOSURES ON ROUTE 87. High stone-wall enclosures were used to segregate agricultural products or as animal pounds for wayward beef cattle, pigs, and sheep. Vestiges of such 18th-century cattle pens are located on Route 87. (CHS.)

CLARKE HOUSE. This gambrel-style farmhouse on Route 87, built around 1742, was once a dairy and sheep farm near Columbia's center. A large well and well sweep and outbuildings are seen in this 1910 postcard. The three large sugar maples that line the front have since been removed. A cottage garden and a quince and lilac thicket surround the farmhouse. (CHS.)

CLARKE HOUSE LYE STONE. A remarkable 18th-century granite lye stone measuring four feet by five feet is positioned on a slight slope within a few yards of the well. Lye was made from wood ashes and water. It was an important ingredient for making soap, using rendered animal fat, in this case from sheep. Lye was also an essential ingredient in the tanning process used by four local tanning houses. (CHS.)

25

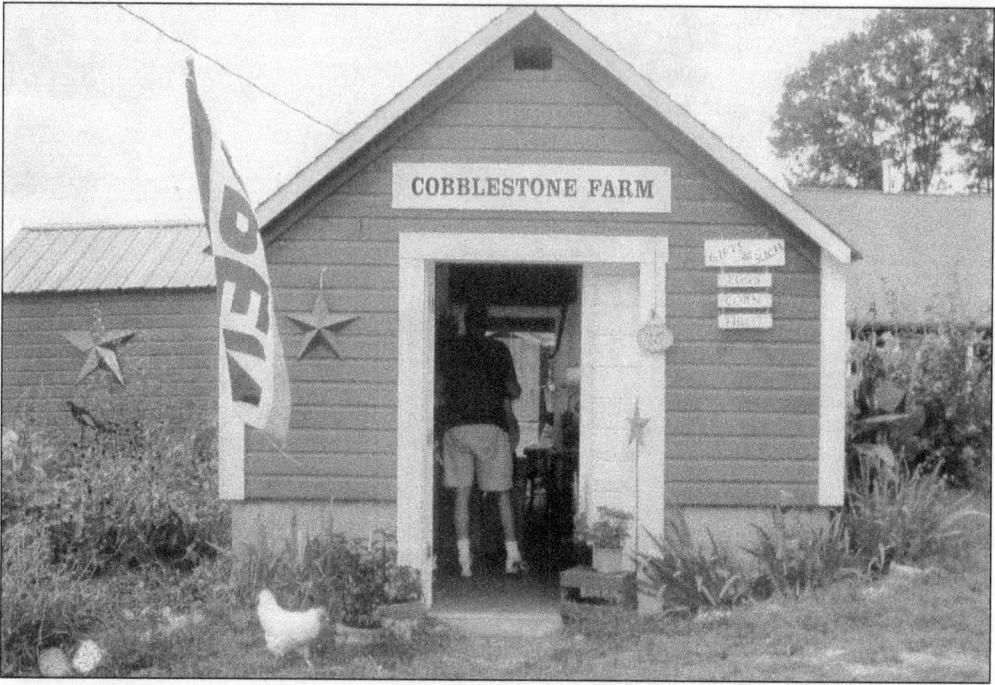

FORMER ICEHOUSE. Until 1930, the preservation of meat, fish, dairy products, and apples required a cool location, such as a well, a well house, a springhouse, or an icehouse. Icehouses were located near ponds, dairy farms, and, later, railroad stations. Icehouses such as the Cobblestone Icehouse and Cherry Valley Icehouse have been converted to modern uses. (CHS.)

ICE-CUTTING ON A COLUMBIA POND. The practice of cutting block ice was a communal activity involving sledges, wagons, and oxen or horses. Nearly all farms had a pond that provided water for cattle in the summer and winter ice for year-round food preservation. Large-scale ice harvesting and storage facilitated commercialization of the local dairy industry in the middle and late 1800s. (CHS.)

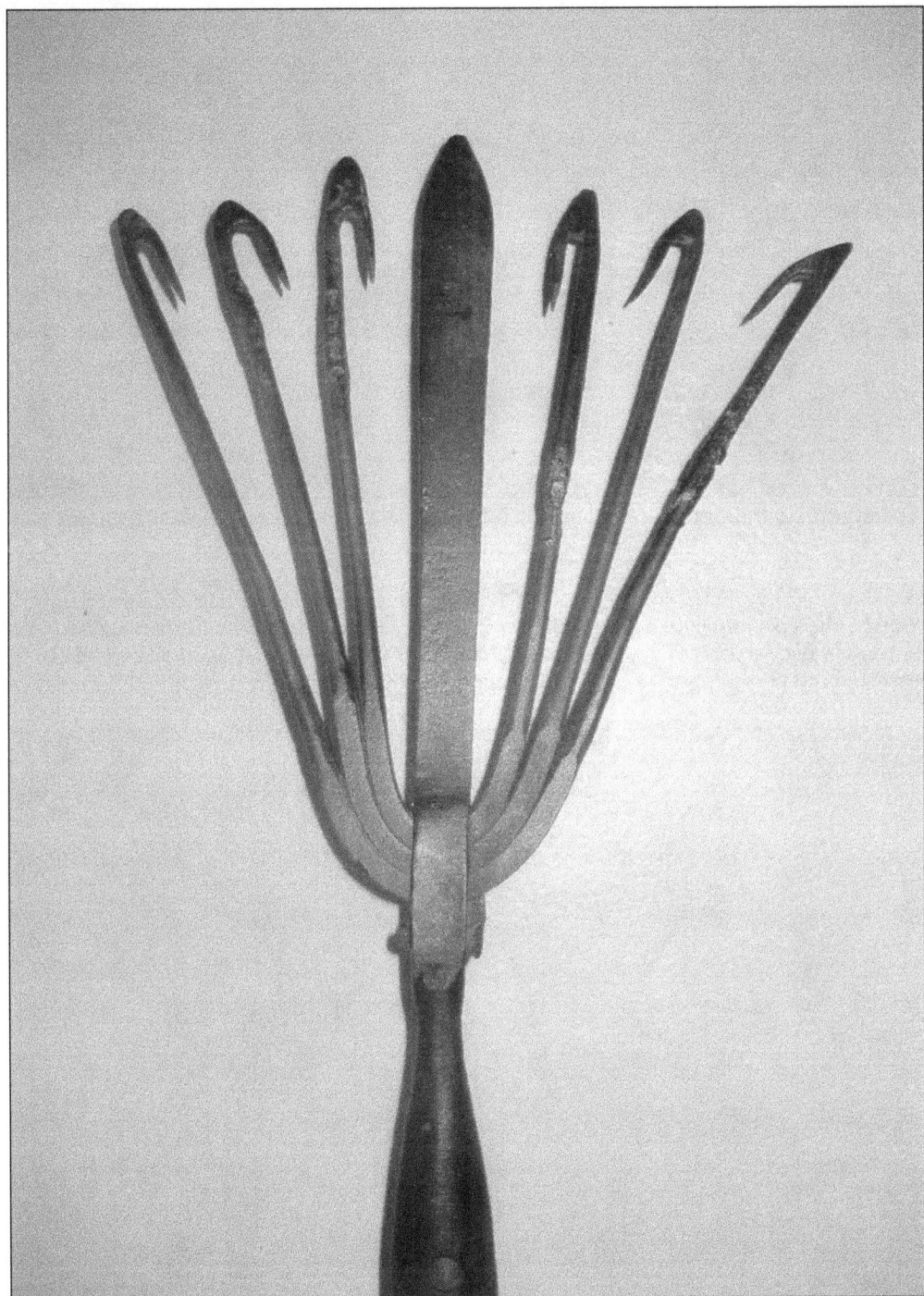

EEL SPEAR. Until 1850, local rivers and streams abounded with shad, herring, trout, and eels. A food staple of both Native Americans and early colonists, eels were fished with forklike spears, which would catch the eels between the tines. New England fisheries exported large quantities of eel to Europe and Asia. Eels are fished by recreational fishermen using a similar device. (Courtesy I. Wood.)

AGRICULTURAL PRODUCTS. A Columbia, Tolland County, inventory of agricultural products and cattle in the late 1850s included: sheep, 1,615; wool, 4,435 pounds; horses, 140; cattle, 910; swine, 364; corn, 7,244 bushels; rye, 1,490 bushels; oats, 5,869 bushels; potatoes, 12,252 bushels; esculents, 1,923 bushels; hay, 1,774 tons; flax, 240 pounds; fruit, 6,621 bushels; tobacco, 1,070 pounds; silk, 4 pounds; butter, 19,148 pounds; cheese, 17,134 pounds; honey, 206 pounds; beeswax, 14 pounds; buckwheat, 895 bushels; beans, 145 bushels; and charcoal, 20,000 bushels. By 1893, as seen in this photograph of farmer J.A. Isham, Columbia remained an agricultural community. (ASBLFL and CHS.)

PALMER GRISTMILL. Built in 1829 for grinding corn and rye with waterpower from a millpond of the Ten Mile River, this gristmill served Columbia and Lebanon families in the Chestnut Hill and Liberty Hill Districts. Here, it serves as the background for a celebratory photograph in 1907. The mill was dismantled in the 1930s, and the stone blocks were reused as roadbed for Route 87. (CHS.)

JUSTIN ISHAM'S CIDER MILL, C. 1910.
The abundance of small apple orchards
reflects the self-sufficiency of the family
farm, as apples were a predictable
cash crop. Even Eleazar Wheelock
maintained a small apple orchard for
cider production in 1760. Isham's cider
mill was located near the junction
of Lake and Erdoni Roads. (CHS.)

**BROWN'S APPLE ORCHARD ON
COLUMBIA RESERVOIR.** Columbia's
farmers experimented with some prize
apple varieties that had already made
neighboring Lebanon famous. In the
early 1900s, apples grown commercially
were transported by rail to urban New
England markets. This site is now a
year-round residential neighborhood
near Columbia Lake beach. (CHS.)

OLD ENGLISH–STYLE BARN. The Old English mixed-use barn was replaced by the New England compartmentalized barn in the mid-1800s. Columbia's 18th-century barns are of the former style, with level-entry side doors. The 19th-century, New England–style barns can be identified by their raised-entry gable-end doors. This photograph shows a former Old English–style barn, built around 1795, now converted to a home on Route 87. (CHS.)

Riverside, Columbia, Conn.

JOHNSON MAPLE SUGAR BUSH. The Johnson Maple Sugar Bush, 133 acres of rock maple trees on Johnson Road, produced upward of 125 gallons of maple syrup a year. The Johnsons sold their "sweet waffle syrup" from their home, Riverside, on the Ten Mile River; by mail order; and at Young and Son's store in Willimantic. Production ceased after the trees were damaged by the 1938 hurricane. (ASBLFL.)

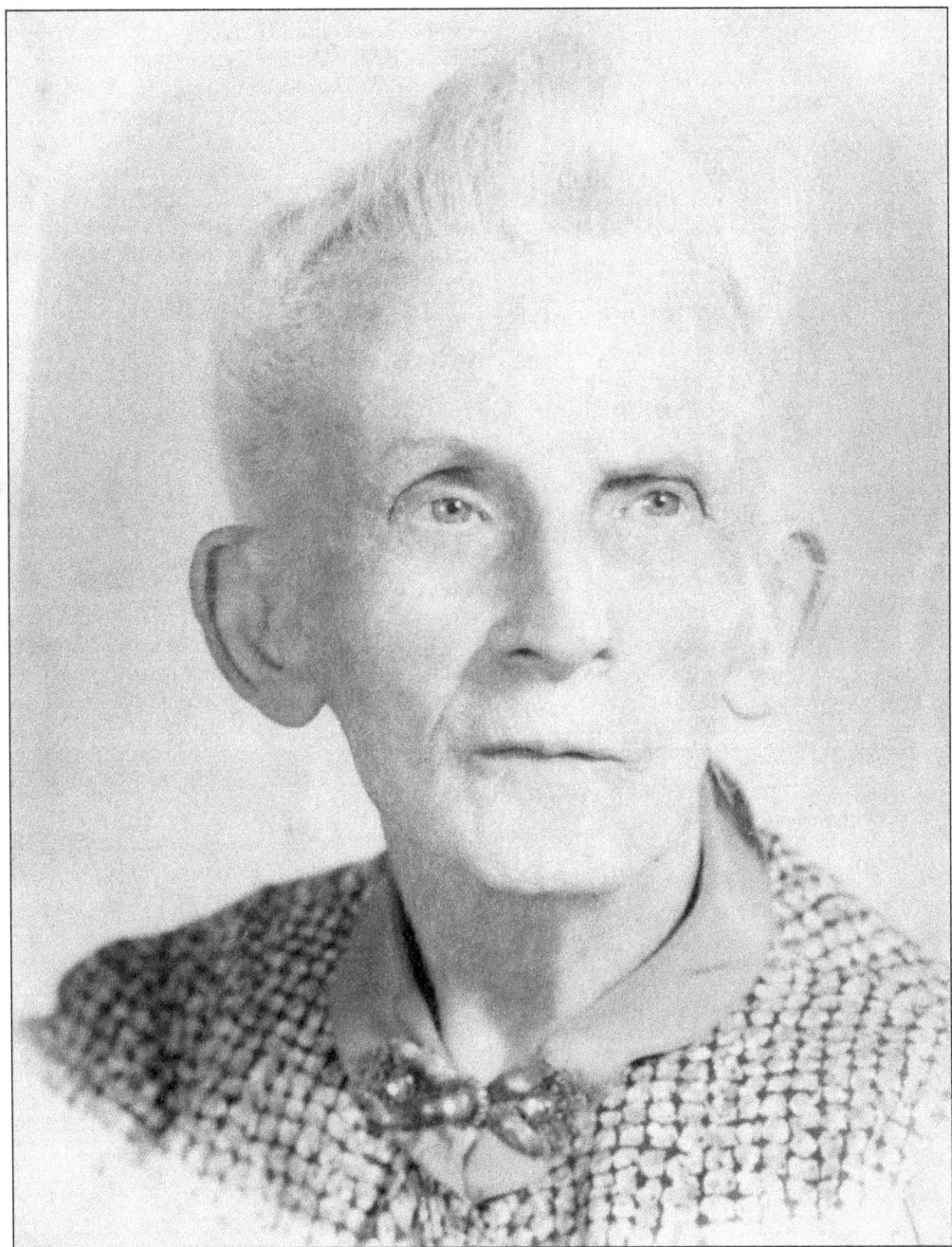

HARRIET FULLER JOHNSON. Harriet Johnson was called "Sweet Grandma." Remembered as gracious hosts, the Johnsons managed the largest sugar bush in Connecticut for 31 years. The sugar bush was maintained by Thomas Traynum of Virginia, a master in the art of maple sugaring. It is now a residential neighborhood. Harriet Johnson's recollection of the Great White Hurricane is immortalized in her account, reprinted in the local Willimantic newspaper. The Blizzard of 1888 created 40- to 50-foot snowdrifts on March 11–14, 1888. It took three weeks for men in her household, using a team of oxen, to dig a way from Riverside Farm to Columbia's center, a distance of three miles. (CHS.)

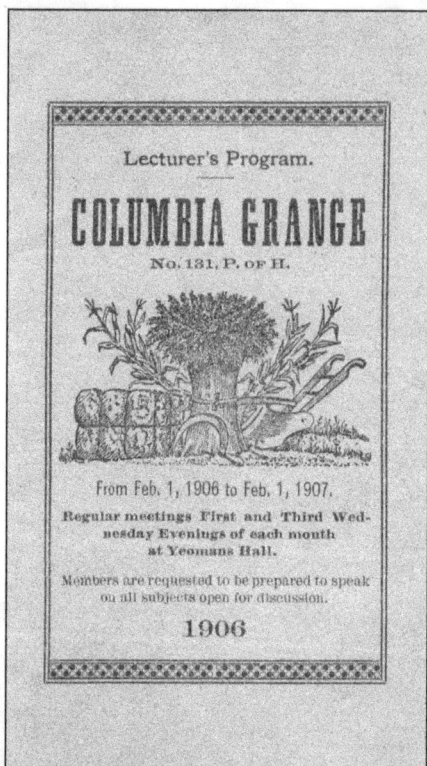

Lecturer's Program.

COLUMBIA GRANGE

No. 131, P. of H.

From Feb. 1, 1906 to Feb. 1, 1907.

Regular meetings First and Third Wednesday Evenings of each month at Yeomans Hall.

Members are requested to be prepared to speak on all subjects open for discussion.

1906

COLUMBIA GRANGE NO. 131. Organized on March 28, 1892, with 35 charter members, Columbia Grange No. 131, Patrons of Husbandry, closed its doors abruptly in February 1992, nearly a century later. The grange had a profound effect on the cultural, educational, and core social institutions of Columbia. This 1906 lecturer's program includes poetry recitations, musical programs, lectures on astronomy, the economics of sheep-raising versus dairy-raising, and debates on taxable property. (CHS.)

MARCH OF DIMES BENEFIT. At a January 1937 March of Dimes Benefit organized by Columbia Grange No. 131, this "trophy" chicken is presented by Joseph Tashlik to raffle winner Irene Parker. Jane Lyman McKeon looks on. Columbia Grange events were held in Yeomans Hall. (CHS.)

YOUNG OXEN, C. 1930. This photograph from the Squier family reveals a gentleman farmer, Raymond Squier, in Sunday attire posing with his young oxen, in training for hard work and future Fourth of July parades. Rambunctious oxen were directed to remarkable trainer Robert Cobb. Oxen were trained and shod and performed all manner of hauling tasks that in later years were performed by heavy engines. (Courtesy Squier Collection; ASBLFL.)

PIG SLAUGHTER, SQUIER HOME, C. 1930. Farm communities such as Columbia in the 1930s depended on their domestic livestock for daily sustenance. Here, a butchered hog is being lowered into boiling water to remove its bristles. Meat was divided among families or processed into smoked products such as bacon or sausage for preservation. (Courtesy Squier Collection; ASBLFL.)

NEW ENGLAND MILK PRODUCERS ASSOCIATION. At the first annual outing of the New England Milk Producers Association (NEMPA), Southern Market District, on August 17, 1938, local dairy farm families are seated on the green. Young Harriet E. Robinson Lyman is seated in the first row, seventh from the right. Small Connecticut dairy farms were considered the most productive

in the nation until the 1950s, when the economics of dairy farming began to favor large-scale production. The successor to the NEMPA, Agri-Mark Incorporated of Methuen, Massachusetts, is now the largest dairy cooperative in New England. The organization markets familiar brands such as Cabot and Hood. (Courtesy I. Wood.)

KAPLAN FAMILY, C. 1929. Columbia's poultry industry, bolstered by successive Eastern European immigrations between 1901 and 1954, was initially aided by the Jewish Agricultural and Industrial Aid Society. The Agricultural College at nearby Storrs, Connecticut, provided assistance to depleted dairy farms and helped the first eight Jewish families create the nascent poultry industry that expanded throughout eastern Connecticut. The Kaplans and other families built the Synagogue Agudath Achim. (ASBLFL.)

HORSES EVERYWHERE! From colonial times to the early 20th century, Columbia's horses provided transportation and power for agricultural tasks and milling. Horse sheds were maintained behind the Columbia Congregational Church as late as the 1930s. This horse is receiving a new shoe during an exhibit on the green. Today, Columbia has 10 equestrian centers offering a range of specialties, including physical therapy development. (ASBLFL and CHS.)

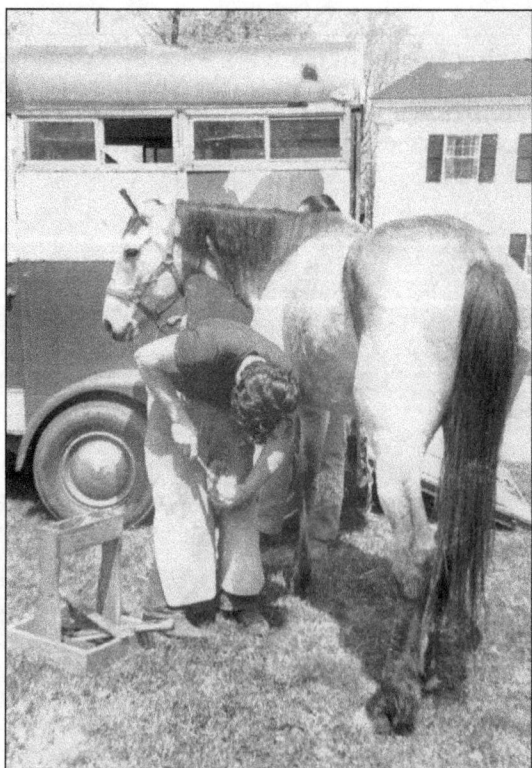

Three

COMMERCE AND INDUSTRY

As early as 1720, gristmills, sawmills, and shingle mills appeared along the Hop and Ten Mile Rivers, followed by a proliferation of mills along every brook that had a grade between eight and nine percent and a continuously flowing stream. The Utley Hill Preserve in the Columbia Lake watershed still contains evidence of five pre–Industrial Revolution mills. Several dams, large earthworks, two flumes, a stone pier, a granite bridge, and one remaining turbine are clues to productivity in the pre–Civil War "Age of Water." At least two of these were gristmills, one with a perpendicular overshot wheel seven feet in diameter to take advantage of the steep grade. The reciprocating motion of the up-and-down sawmill was once powered by 14 "orange peel" turbines. First-growth forests of oak, beech, pine, chestnut, and maple were harvested to produce lumber, barrel staves, spindles, shingles, and splints. The 1860 census lists eight water-powered sawmills and two water-powered shingle mills. By 1870, however, efficient steam-powered sawmill technology began to replace waterpower. Lumber was used throughout the region to build barns, houses, and churches, as well as in the construction of industrial structures such as railroad facilities, woodturning mills, tanneries, a piano factory, a wagon and sleigh factory, a broom factory, a cotton mill, and a basket manufacturer. Columbia's rye and corn were milled into flour and animal meal, and apples were pressed for juice and cider. Columbia also had two sorghum mills. Sorghum, an ancient African grain, was made into sorghum molasses and mash. These comestibles were consumed locally. Columbia's early-1800s merino sheep-raising experiment expanded wool processing, necessitating carding and fulling mills, which used seasonal waterpower. The 1850 census shows eight hat factories producing 47,000 woolen plantation hats valued at $19,016. The Hop River Warp Company (1838–1912) was the first large-scale industrial cotton mill in Connecticut, owned successively by E. Smith, A. Dunham, and A. and W. Jillson. The Hop River Village was organized as a model mill village. Columbia Manufacturing Inc., specializing in aircraft industry fabrications, is the only major manufacturing presence today.

KOZELKA FAMILY MONUMENT. This one-piece, dressed, revolving runner stone was likely sourced in Narragansett, Rhode Island. Such scored millstones were intended for grinding cornmeal. Columbia gristmills had at least two types of waterwheels: undershot for low waterfalls, and the less common overshot for high waterfalls, as in the Utley Hill Preserve. (CHS.)

SPILLWAY, C. 1920. The spillway at the Ravine once provided water for the early Lyman Tannery in 1783 and for the Norman P. Little Hat Factory in 1850. At its lower reach, near Route 6, was once a millpond and water-powered sawmill. In 1865, American Thread Company dammed a pond that became Columbia Reservoir and used the Ravine to control water levels for its mills along the Willimantic River. (CHS.)

COLUMBIA CENTER, LOOKING WEST, C. 1896. Two millponds, a sawmill, a tanning house, and a blacksmith shop were located in the Center District, along what was variously called Old Hebron Road, Middletown Turnpike, Route 6A, and now Route 66. Note the absence of trees and the presence of telephone or telegraph poles. Telephone service was introduced in 1891. (CHS.)

39

EDWARD LYMAN PLOWING SNOW, RT. 87

EDWARD LYMAN "PLOWING" SNOW. In 1869, four tanneries produced all manner of leather goods, such as harnesses, saddles, boots, shoes, hinges, straps, breeches for men, skirts for women, and blackjacks—leather drinking mugs, pitchers, and bottles. Tanneries required an ample water supply, milled spruce or hemlock bark, lye, and large vats. A single circular millstone powered by a horse was used to mill tree bark. (CHS.)

HOP RIVER DEPOT. This depot served passengers and freight and operated as a post office and as a transfer point for raw material for the Hop River Mill complex, Connecticut's oldest industrial cotton mill. The station house was later moved to a nearby site on Hop River Road in Coventry, where it served as a residence. Though now unpainted and seemingly abandoned, it is still recognizable, with its metal roof. The Hop River Mill complex, built in 1837, originally produced yarns, threads, and warps. It also manufactured machine tools for cotton opening. William Jillson renovated the mill in 1882–1885 to include a steam engine and boiler for additional power, apartments, and a schoolhouse. In 1898, the complex included the Moosewood Silk Company, and in 1910 and 1911, the Case Leatherboard Company and American Board Company produced leather, seating, and paper products. (UCONN.)

GHOST TRAIN. The fabled white train officially named "The New England Limited" sped through small towns, including Columbia, during early evening at speeds up to 60 miles per hour, traversing the 213 miles of track from New York to Boston. Starting on March 16, 1891, and ending on October 20, 1895, trains left both terminals daily at 3:00 p.m. and arrived at 9:00 p.m. The New England Limited inspired Rudyard Kipling's poem "Ghost Train:"

Without a jar, or roll or antic, Without a stop to Willimantic,
The New England Limited takes its way
At three o'clock on every day.
Maids and matrons, daintily dinited,
Ride every day on the New England
Limited;
Rain or snow ne'er stops its flight,
It makes New York at nine each night.
One half of the glories have not been
Told
Of that wonderful train of white and
Gold
Which leaves every day for New York
At Three
Over the N.Y. and N.E.

(UCONN.)

THE TRAVELING SAWMILL, C. 1908. A portable steam-powered sawmill owned by George Little (seated behind the young boy and dog at center) was deployed throughout New England. Columbia's lumbermen pose at a Claremont, New Hampshire, camp. Winter was typically peak logging season. Mechanized steam-powered sawmills represented a technological innovation, directly accessing inland forests and using scrap wood as a fuel source for the boiler. Standing here are, from left to right, Mason Squier, Abbot Little, Fred Duschane, Bill Nuhfer, four unidentified men, and baseball player Willis Richards. The young boy with the dog in the foreground is Horace Little. (Courtesy Nancy Nuhfer.)

BASKET SHOP FACTORY. Norman P. Little (seated at center) started a basket-weaving factory in 1865 using the skills he learned from Native Americans. Soon, his shop on Basket Shop Road employed 18 men. Baskets were transported to Hartford by horse and wagon and then to the Hop River Depot for shipment by rail. The business was sold to Abraham Lavietes, who moved the operation to Shelton, Connecticut, in 1910. Seen here after his retirement is Little and his family in East Hartford. (ASBLFL.)

THE AGE OF STEAM. One day in July 1958, Marshall Squier's very large, c. 1910 antique steam tractor appeared on a hill just west of Columbia's center on Route 66. He said he bought it because his father, Raymond Squier, had once owned a similar machine, called a steam traction engine. It was built by International Harvester, weighed between eight and nine tons, and required three men or a smaller tractor to crank-start. (ASBLFL.)

COLUMBIA CENTER, C. 1930. Taken from the open cockpit of Marshall Squier's Waco-made biplane, "Peola," this photograph shows Columbia Center, Hop River, and Cards Mill Districts. Note the unusual, elongated town green bounded by the Congregational Church, original Yeomans Hall, white clapboard houses, farms, the Landmark, and Old Yard Burying Ground. The Center Burying Ground in the lower right is surrounded by open pasture. In 1930, Columbia's population was at an all-time low of 648. The biplane was hangared in Clarke's barn, which blew down during the hurricane of 1938. The damaged biplane was sold, repaired, and last sighted on exhibit at the Rhinebeck, New York, aerodrome. (ASBLFL.)

COLUMBIA'S INVENTIVE GENIUS. Tressillian "Tinker" Tucker ran a machine shop near 203 Route 66. He started out with a small steam-powered sawmill and a wood-turning and woodworking shop. He turned his legendary mechanical ability and electrical knowledge to automotive applications. He later created engineered prototypes for the University of California and Amherst College. As a youngster in 1886, he built a camera, and he later set up the first electric lights in Columbia, using batteries. He owned the first high-wheeled bicycle, first motorcycle, and first automobile in town. In 1907, he established an automobile repair shop for New England clients well before the first blacktop appeared in Columbia in 1917. This studio photograph, the only one of its kind in the Columbia Historical Society Collection, shows a young man, possibly Tressillian Tucker, with his high-wheeled bicycle. (CHS.)

46

POST OFFICE AND RESIDENCE OF G. B. FULLER, COLUMBIA, CONN.

PUB. BY AMELIA I. FULLER.

TENNANT, PHOTO.

POST OFFICE AND RESIDENCE OF G.B. FULLER, C. 1900. This postcard shows Columbia's post office (at left) on the green. The view is to the northeast from the Landmark at what is now the intersection of Routes 66 and 87. Note the horse and carriage and unpaved road in front. This structure was known as the Fuller's Store and the first Porter Store. It was moved to widen the intersection during Columbia's 1930s road-building era. (CHS.)

POST OFFICE AND PORTER STORE, C. 1935. The second Porter Store and post office were resurrected in a barn that was built by Horace W. Porter. As the population grew in the 1950s, a separate post office was built. Porter Store was succeeded by Smith's Store, Keegan's General Store, and Don and Suzanne Doborowlsky's store, called Don's Market. This building was demolished in the late 1990s. (Courtesy of Nancy Nuhfer.)

THE LANDMARK, LEWIS STORE, AND GAS STATION, C. 1930. This general store, pharmacy, and luncheonette were demolished in the mid-1930s to widen the intersection of Routes 66 and 87. At that time, the building at right, the Landmark (formerly an 18th-century inn) was the Squier residence. Its upstairs "floating" ballroom was rented out to various organizations and became headquarters for Columbia's British War Relief Effort from 1939 to 1941. (CHS.)

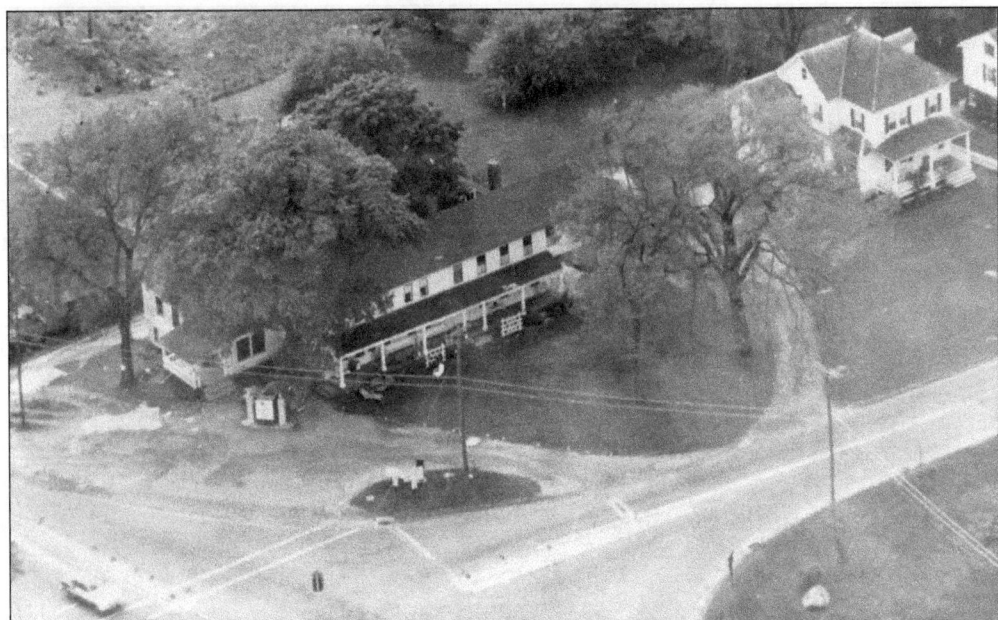

THE LANDMARK. The southwest corner of the intersection of Routes 66 and 87 can be seen from this aerial photograph taken sometime before 1962. The Landmark barns and outbuildings were burned in January 1963 to make way for a new parking area for the Beckish Pharmacy. Marshall Squier sold the Landmark to Frances and Peter Beckish of Willimantic in April 1963. Note the pasture behind the houses. (ASBLFL.)

BECKISH PHARMACY AT THE LANDMARK, C. 1963. Frances and Peter Beckish remodeled Squier's store to open Columbia's first pharmacy and soda fountain. Peter Beckish was a pharmacist. The Landmark was sold to the Ramm family by Tom Welles in 1992. The Beckish family's legacy was a gift of land for the Beckish Senior Center. (ASBLFL.)

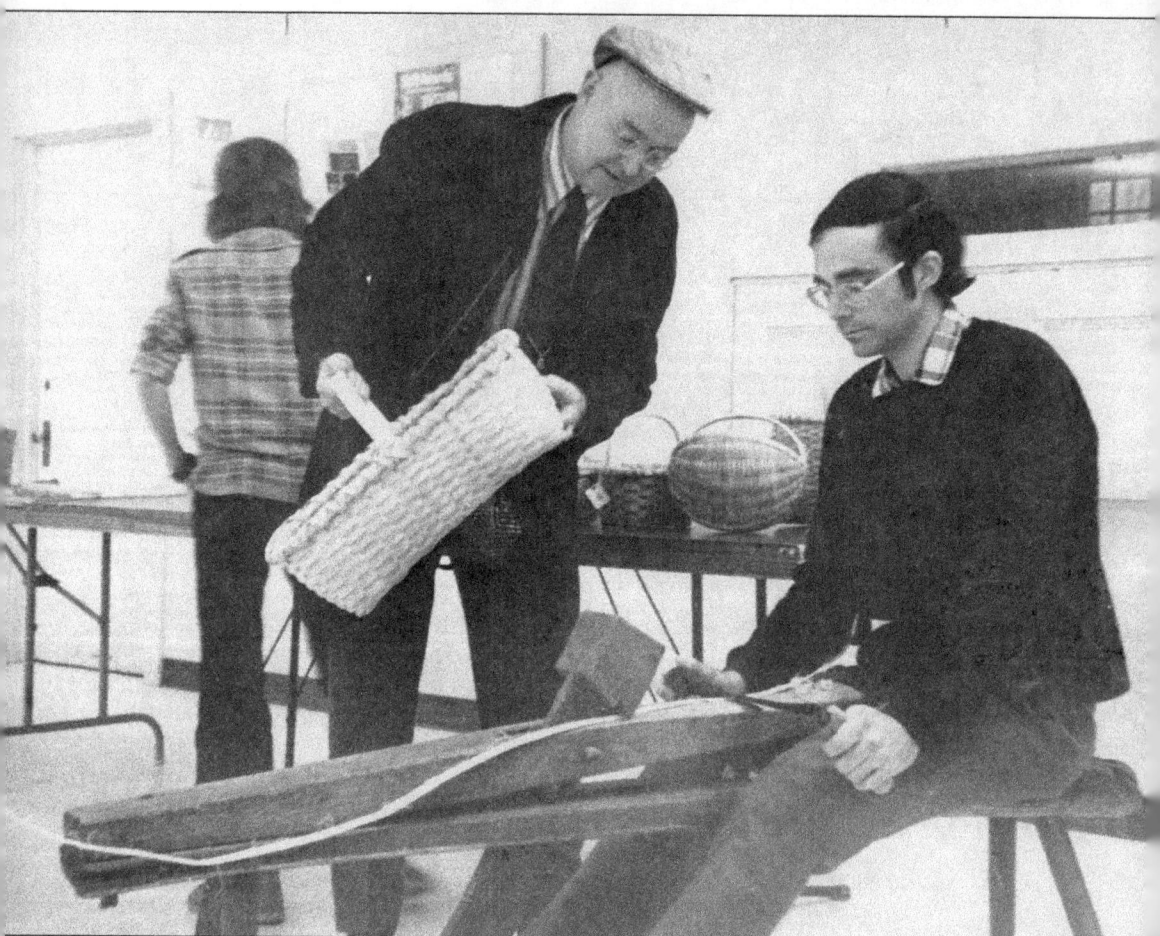

FROM PLANTATION HATS TO BASKETS. Columbia's frenetic pre–Civil War industries came to an abrupt halt with Emancipation and the Age of Steam. The eight water-powered carding and fulling mills used for the production of large quantities of plantation hats were abandoned. One mill, repurposed by Norman P. Little for basket making, served in that capacity until 1910, when Little sold his business. Seen here is a Little-style basket with interesting handles woven into the basket for durability. A published, unedited inventory of industry and industrial products in Columbia, undertaken by the Tolland County, Connecticut, census in the late 1850s, includes:

Industry and Products Manufactured (pre–Civil War):
Cotton Mill, 1; spindles, 765; cotton consumed, 46,800 lbs.; cotton yarn manufactured, 42,744 lbs.
Hat and Cap Factories, 8; number manufactured, 47,000; valued at $19,016.
Wagon and Sleigh Factory, 1; value of manufactures, $1,425.
Boots manufactured, 320 pairs; shoes manufactured, 170 pairs; valued at $664.
Stone quarried, valued at $225.
Wooden-ware manufactured, valued at $92.
Brooms manufactured, 1,614; valued at $225.
Lumber prepared for market, 280,000 feet; valued at $2,830.
Firewood prepared for market, 424 cords; valued at $896.

(ASBLFL.)

Four

TO LEARN AND TO PRAY

The first families of the new proprietorship based their lives around home and church. By 1720, Lebanon's Second Ecclesiastical Society had been established. Rev. Samuel Smith was settled as the first pastor. The first covenant was signed by Nehemiah Closson, Josiah Dewey, Nathaniel House, John Hutchinson, Josiah Loomys, Richard Lyman, John Newcomb, James Pineaux, Samuel Smith, John Sullard, John Swetland, George Way, Benjamin Woodworth, and Samuel Wright. The meetinghouse was seated January 10, 1733, and by 1751, a successor meetinghouse had been seated. Administration of town affairs remained inseparable from the church until 1818. Church records show that in 1804, when Columbia was incorporated, the town's new officers continued to meet in the Congregational meetinghouse until a separate town administrative office was built in 1835. By 1832, the third and present Congregational meetinghouse had been seated. In time, denominations of other faiths established their own permanent presence. Congregation Agudath Achim, formed in 1927, built its synagogue in 1952. The first Roman Catholic services were held in various locations until 1944, when a residence near the green was purchased and consecrated as St. Columba Roman Catholic Chapel to serve residents of Columbia, Andover, and Hebron. A new St. Columba Roman Catholic Church was built at the site in 1955. In 1970, the Cooper family donated land on Route 6 for the Baptist Fellowship Church, which was built the following year.

By 1865, Columbia had seven school districts, each with a one-room school. The schools were publicly maintained by the town's School Society and overseen by the Board of School Visitors. An eighth district, Hop River Village School, was built in 1885. All districts were consolidated in 1948 into one central school, Horace W. Porter School, serving first through eighth grades. An ever-expanding number of high schools and technical schools were established in neighboring Windham, Storrs-Mansfield, Bolton, Lebanon, and now Norwich. In 1739, a library jointly owned by local citizens, called the Philogrammatician Society, was maintained by Rev. Solomon Williams. In 1883, The Columbia Free Library was founded. A larger structure was dedicated in 1903 and again in 1985 as the Saxton B. Little Free Library.

WEST STREET SCHOOLHOUSE, C. 1935. Built in 1853, this school was originally located north of the intersection with Basket Shop Road. In 1889, the Connecticut school year was increased from 30 to 36 weeks, constituting three terms. Rural Columbia objected, insisting that its young people were needed for planting and harvest season. Records show that West Street School District existed as early as 1768. The decommissioned school building was incorporated into a nearby house. (CHS.)

PINE STREET SCHOOL, C. 1948. Teacher extraordinaire Ethel Brehant, seen here with her pupils, is still fondly remembered as Pine Street's longtime inspiration. This one-room school was rebuilt in 1884. Attendance records from 1859 to 1865 show a winter term (November to early March) and a summer term (late April to August). An earlier building was once located at the intersection of Hunt Road and Pine Street. (CHS.)

OLD HOP RIVER SCHOOLHOUSE, C. 1910. Built in 1744 on land donated by Josiah Finney, the schoolhouse was extended in 1923. It once stood near Old Willimantic and Cherry Valley Roads. The Old Hop River District was one of three public school districts mentioned in 1739 Ecclesiastical Society records. The Congregational Church relinquished all responsibility for schools in 1797, when the administrative School Society was established. (CHS.)

OLD HOP RIVER SCHOOL STUDENTS, 1895. Master A.E. Lyman (rear left) is seen with his pupils. By 1737, the system of rotating "masters" to teach writing and reading, and "dames" to teach reading the rest of the year, was being employed. This method lasted until statewide standards were legislated in 1872. Columbia's elected Board of Visitors was required to evaluate each school to ascertain if it met requirements for annual state and local funding. (CHS.)

HOP RIVER VILLAGE SCHOOLHOUSE, C. 1900. Built in 1885 by William Jillson, owner of Hop River Warp Company, this was the last one-room school to be built in Columbia's new Eighth District. It was part of Jillson's vision of a model mill village. The Carpenter Gothic Revival structure had two entrances. It was converted to commercial offices, and is now a private residence. The large school bell was donated to the Columbia Historical Society. (CHS.)

CHESTNUT HILL SCHOOLHOUSE INTERIOR, C. 1913. Located on the northwest corner of Route 87 and Doubleday and Latham Roads, this building was moved to private property in the 1930s. In the 1920s, the curriculum changed from the mastery of reading, writing, and arithmetic skills to the Project Method, a precursor of the Progressive Educational Movement, which focused on child readiness, creative problem-solving, and classroom learning as microcosm. (CHS.)

54

NORTH DISTRICT SCHOOL, C. 1914. Located on Whitney Road, North District School was moved in 1866 following the creation of the American Thread Company reservoir the previous year. The students, pictured here with teacher Marion Lyman Hurlbutt (in doorway) are, from left to right, Mason Nuhfer, Margaret Krozel, Donald Woodward, Evelyn Lyman, Evelyn Woodward, Helen Brown, Josephine Krozel, Chauncey Squier, Howard Squier, Marshall Squier, and Harold Woodward. (CHS.)

CENTER SCHOOLHOUSE, C. 1948. Center School has moved four times, and is now at its fifth and current location, on the green. It served as Moor's Indian Charity School from 1755 to 1769, was Lebanon Crank's Center School by 1778, and remained in use as an overflow classroom for Horace W. Porter students as late as 1956. It is currently maintained as a one-room school museum by the Town of Columbia and the Columbia Historical Society. (CHS.)

WINDHAM HIGH SCHOOL "BUS," C. 1915. Columbia high school students were conveyed to nearby Windham High School in winter by horse-drawn sleigh, a standard means of winter transportation, until 1917, when the town purchased an adapted REO truck. Students also used the local train at the Chestnut Hill, Leonard's Bridge, Hop River, and Andover stations for daily transportation to Windham High. (CHS.)

NIGHT SCHOOL, C. **1930.** From 1927 to 1933, the board of education conducted citizenship and language training at night for newly immigrated, foreign-born adults at the Center School. This wave of immigration from England, Austria, Hungary, Poland, Ukraine, Belarus, and Lithuania was the result of increasing unrest and economic crisis in Europe. All emigration from central European Soviet bloc countries was abruptly curtailed in 1928 by Stalin's New Economic Policy. Columbia's night school attendance began to fall off by 1931, and classes ceased in 1933. Shown here are, from left to right, (first row) unidentified, Millie Bitten, Myer Bitten, and Abraham Tannenbaum; (second row) Esther Kresowitz, Frank Postemsky, Celia Kresowitz, and Mrs. Kresowitz; (third row) unidentified, and Mr. and Mrs. Price; (fourth row) Alexander Zuryk, Olga Zuryk, Mary Zuryk, and unidentified; (standing in rear) Superintendent Garrison, and school committee members Junie Squier and Fannie Dixon Welch. Standing at the chalkboard is instructor Madeline Holmes Mitchell. Mary Zuryk played the song "America" on the button box accordion for each night school graduating class. (CHS.)

HORACE W. PORTER SCHOOL, C. 1948. Initially serving 150 students, the Horace Porter School required expansion by 1958. Seen here is the class of 1956, some of whose members fondly recall studying in the one-room overflow building, Center School next door. Supervising principal George Patros (1953–1966) oversaw three expansion projects, and by the end of his tenure, enrollment reached 603 students. (ASBLFL.)

HORACE W. PORTER EXPANSION, C. 1993. Town officials ready their shovels for a commemorative "dig" for yet another school addition. Performing the honors on October 16, 1993, are, from left to right, public works officer Angelo Casale, architect Jim Cassidy, First Selectman Adella Urban, school building committee representative John Lauer, chairman of the board of education Alan Giordano, contractor Keith Nasin, and Supt. Dean Toepfer. (ASBLFL.)

COLUMBIA FREE LIBRARY, C. 1883. The 320-square-foot public library opened on December 14, 1883. The tradition that preceded it includes Lebanon's 1739 Philogrammatician Society, the Propriatory Library of Lebanon Crank (1797–1825), and the Franklin Library (1830–1857). Saxton B. Little and residents of seven school districts donated funds for construction, maintenance, and endowment, totaling $1,376 and $184.40 in in-kind labor. (CHS.)

LIBRARY COMMITTEE, 1902. Chaired by businessman and civic leader Joseph Hutchins in 1900, the Library Committee proposed an expansion or the construction of a new library. Hutchins financed $2,246.68 of the total cost of $2,746.12 for a new building. Total donations, including a $500 gift from Saxton B. Little, amounted to $3,084.68. The site, a 45-by-45-foot plot across Center Cemetery Lane from the original 1883 library, was also donated by Hutchins. (ASBLFL.)

William H. Yeomans.   Amelia J. Fuller.   William A. Collins.

Joseph Hutchins   Alanson H. Fox.   James P. Little.

Library Committee 1902.

SAXTON BAILEY LITTLE. Born in Columbia, Saxton B. Little (1813–1907) became a schoolteacher at the Pine Street School. In 1844, he left Columbia to teach at the State School for Boys in Meriden, Connecticut, where he developed a method for teaching mathematics that became the basis for an early mathematics workbook. He was a major benefactor of two successive Columbia libraries. This studio photograph was taken on July 31, 1888. (CHS.)

FORMER SAXTON B. LITTLE FREE LIBRARY, C. 1985. Dedicated on June 17, 1903, this Queen Anne building, designed by Wilton Little of Willimantic, was reproduced in other Connecticut towns. The stately reading room now serves as *The Meeting Place* conference room. With limited space and few amenities, the facility could not provide services to meet a population that had expanded from 655 in 1900 to 3,386 in 1980. By 1977, library expansion was under discussion. (ASBLFL.)

Saxton B. Little Free Library Renovation, c. 1983. Formerly an 18th-century inn, the residence of longtime Columbia teacher and librarian Gladys Rice Soracchi became the third home of Saxton B. Little's vision for a public library. Seen here under renovation in the early 1980s, the new library opened on November 24, 1985, at a cost of $472,000. It is supported by the town, the state, and endowment funds. (ASBLFL.)

Saxton B. Little Free Library, c. 1985. Originally envisaged to house over 20,000 volumes, the library now serves 5,000 residents and houses 57,000 items. It hosts after-school programs for youngsters and evening seminars for adults. It is connected through interlibrary loan to major research libraries and the Connecticut public library system. The Friends of the Library was organized in 1977 to provide financial support, advocacy, outreach, and expanded services to the community. (ASBLFL.)

EAST SIDE OF COLUMBIA GREEN,
COLUMBIA, CONN.

COLUMBIA CONGREGATIONAL UNITED CHURCH OF CHRIST. The Second Ecclesiastical Society of Lebanon's North Parish oversaw administrative functions such as tax collection and public schools as early as 1720. The parish was founded to serve the preeminent mission of the church. In 1753, Eleazar Wheelock wrote his pastorate's mission, as expressed by Charles II's Royal Charter of the Colony of Connecticut: to spread God's word in this wilderness. (CHS.)

Mr. *Henry Hutchins* Dr. To

The Columbia Congregational Society

For Rent of Pew No. 20 for the year ending Oct. 31, 1907

Amt. $12.00

Received Payment,

E. L. Lyman Collector.

Nov 5 1907

ANNUAL PEW RENTAL, 1907. The 18th-century tradition of seating of the meetinghouse was determined by a venerable committee of the Columbia Congregational Society. Seating was appointed by age, estate, or office. This tradition gradually evolved into pew rentals, as seen in this Columbia Congregational Church form for pew no. 20, rented to Henry Hutchins for the annual amount of $12 in 1907. (ASBLFL.)

COLUMBIA CONGREGATIONAL CHURCH. This third meetinghouse, on Columbia's green, was built in Greek Revival style in 1832 by the Webler and Newell Company of Wells Woods. In 1868, and again in 1938, the steeple was toppled. During the hurricane of 1938, the steeple fell point down, bell intact. Seen here is the 1940 reconstruction of the steeple. Of note is the original Yeomans Hall, which burned down in November of that year. (CHS.)

CONGREGATION AGUDATH ACHIM. The Agudath Achim Society (translated from Hebrew, "Society of Brothers, Hand in Hand") was founded by 10 families in 1921. The first temple, located on Chestnut Hill at Latham Hill Road and Route 87, was consecrated in 1927 and rebuilt in 1951, as seen here. The new synagogue was dedicated in 1952 by Chairman Joseph Tashlik. It continues to be used on High Holy Days and special occasions. (ASBLFL.)

St. Columba Roman Catholic Chapel, c. 1944. This Greek Revival house, located across from the Landmark, was dedicated in July 1944 as St. Columba Chapel, serving the Roman Catholic community of Columbia and Andover. It operated under the sponsorship of Saint Joseph's Parish of Willimantic. (CHS.)

St. Columba Roman Catholic Church. Dedicated on May 23, 1955, the new church served Columbia's 126 Catholic families and 85 vacationing lake residents as well as the Roman Catholic community of Andover and Hebron. A sixth-century carved stone from the ancient Abbey of Iona, the famous monastic center founded by Columba in 563, was a gift of the Episcopal Church of Hartford. This church is a parish of the Catholic Diocese of Norwich. (Courtesy I. Wood.)

Baptist Fellowship Church. Dedicated in 1971 under the leadership of Pastor Jack Schneider, the Baptist Fellowship is a regional church serving the nearby towns of Bolton, Coventry, Andover, Hebron, and Mansfield. The church offers fellowship study and prayer, outreach, youth camps, a food pantry, fitness training, and nursing home visits. The site was donated by Lester and Grace Cooper in 1970. (Courtesy Baptist Fellowship Church.)

HOUSES OF WORSHIP IN COLUMBIA

Columbia's Houses of Worship, c. 1975. This composite postcard is meant to convey the major religious denominations in Columbia. Shown are, clockwise from lower left, the Baptist Fellowship Church, St. Columba Roman Catholic Church, Columbia Congregational United Church of Christ, Congregation Agudath Achim Synagogue, and Jehovah's Witnesses Kingdom Hall. (CHS.)

65

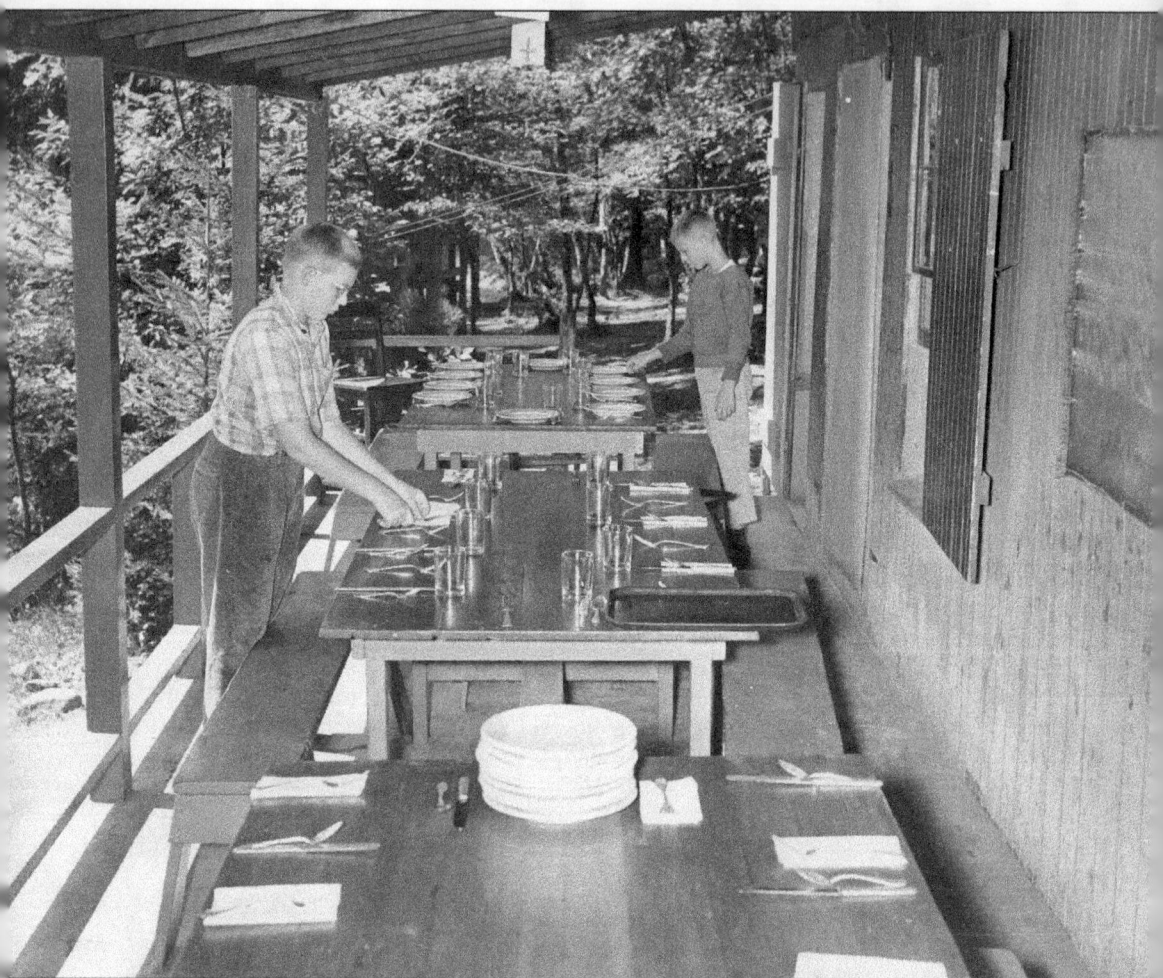

CAMP ASTO WAMAH, C. 1930. The Center Church of Hartford ministry at Columbia Lake reservoir started in 1909. The camp was officially founded as a youth camp and retreat for the First Church of Christ of Hartford in 1910, and the property was purchased in 1914. An adjoining parcel was purchased by the trustees of Hartford's Warburton Chapel. Shown here is preparation for 5:30 p.m. supper at the lodge. The activities included morning prayers and fellowship, swimming, sailing, archery, baseball, outdoor crafts, chores, camp duties, and evening vespers. Campers rose to reveille at 6:30 a.m. and went to sleep after taps at 9:00 p.m. The camp's motto is "Remember the Other Fellow." Generations of families have attended Connecticut's oldest youth camp. (Courtesy N. Mclean.)

Five

SUMMER PLEASURES AND ACTIVITIES AT THE LAKE

One of the major recreational attractions in the town of Columbia is the lake. It is hard to imagine that, prior to 1865, it was a large, swampy wetland. The impetus for the lake came about as a result of the Civil War. Union troops needed clothes, and the American Thread Company of Willimantic, manufacturer of cotton thread, became essential to the war effort. The power source used to run the mill came from the Willimantic River. This source was unreliable, particularly in the summer during periods of drought. The search for additional water to supplement the Willimantic River led to Columbia's wetlands area. The land was acquired and a dam was built to form a reservoir. However, it too was found to be inadequate, as the drainage into the Willimantic River only lasted a short time until the reservoir drained out. This problem, and the advent of electricity, soon rendered the reservoir obsolete. In 1933, the reservoir, now called a lake by locals, was sold to the town for $25,000. The lake soon became a great place to swim, boat, and fish. Visitors and renters came from Hartford and Willimantic on the train, which stopped at the Hop River Station. From there, the travelers walked to the lake. As the years passed, the lake became a summer resort destination. Among the prominent and famous people who built homes on its shores were artist Edith Sawyer; Democratic political and social entertainer Fannie Dixon Welch; Phillip Lauter, owner of the Electro-Motive Company of Willimantic, and his wife, Josephine, a vaudeville entertainer and singer; and June Norcross, founder of Norcross Greeting Cards. Today, the lake is as busy as ever. Swimming lessons for the youth, a gathering spot for teens, fishing and boating, or just soaking in the sun on a towel or chair are a few of the offerings of this eastern Connecticut gem.

AMERICAN THREAD COMPANY. The American Thread Company was indirectly responsible for the formation of Columbia Lake. The firm was established in Willimantic by Lawson C. Ives and Austin Dunham in 1854 to process flax into linen towels. Foreseeing the Civil War, the company switched to producing cotton thread. Six-ply thread was produced at the factory, which had a daily output of 4,000 pounds, or 50,000 spools per week. (Courtesy John Allen.)

WILLIMANTIC RIVER. This river, a tributary of the Shetucket River, is approximately 25 miles long. Before flowing south to the city of Willimantic, the Hop River and Ten Mile River in Columbia flow into it. The Willimantic River drops over 90 feet in one mile and provided an excellent head of pressure to power the mills in Willimantic. (Courtesy John Allen.)

COLUMBIA LAKE, FROM BROWN'S PASTURE. COLUMBIA, CONN.

THE RESERVOIR. During summers, the Willimantic River was an unreliable power source for the mills, which sat idle when the river was low. Supplemental water sources were sought. The pond, wetland, and low-lying, spring-fed areas in Columbia were selected for a reservoir. This photograph shows Brown's pasture, near the present location of the beach. (ASBLFL.)

COLUMBIA DAM SITE. The American Thread Company of Willimantic bought approximately 375 acres from willing and unwilling landowners and dammed the low-lying area to form a reservoir. A few brooks, springs, and rainwater fed the reservoir. The dam was built near the outlet of the lake, now called the Ravine. (ASBLFL.)

Columbia Dam Site

THE DAM.   COLUMBIA. CONN.

EARLY DAM VIEW. This photograph was taken in 1921 from the edge of the lake. The dam, of earthen construction, is 300 feet long and 16 feet wide at the top. Built in 1865 by 25 laborers and five teams of horses, it has withstood the onslaught of every hurricane and severe storm that has torn through Columbia over the past 148 years. (ASBLFL.)

Entrance to Lake.   COLUMBIA, Conn.

TOWN BUYS THE RESERVOIR. After construction of the dam, it was found that water diverted into the Hop River via the reservoir to feed the Willimantic River was insufficient. When electricity came into use shortly thereafter, the American Thread Company had no more use for the reservoir, which was sold to the town for $25,000 in 1933. This early photograph shows a road entrance to the lake. (ASBLFL.)

COLUMBIA LAKE, CONN., FROM BUELL HOMESTEAD.

COLUMBIA LAKE NEAR UTLEY HILL. This photograph shows a view of Columbia Lake from the Buell homestead. This area was one of the first to get electric power. Note the electric power post along the dirt road. The road was then called West Street, and the cemetery was named after it. (ASBLFL.)

COLUMBIA LAKE, FROM WOODWARD HILL. COLUMBIA, CONN.

COLUMBIA LAKE FROM WOODWARD HILL. This postcard shows the lake from Woodward Hill, located north of the dam off Route 87. This area was noted for an early tavern with two large beehive ovens. The Woodward family owned much of this property. William H. Woodward was the secretary of Dartmouth College in 1815. (ASBLFL.)

71

THE RAVINE.   COLUMBIA, CONN.

THE RAVINE. This photograph shows the outlet of the lake, called the Ravine, running at full capacity. When the water level of the lake gets too high, a gate is opened to maintain the lake at a safe level. The water flows into the Hop River. The primary source feeding the lake is the Columbia Lake Brook, which flows into the lake near the junction of Lake and Erdoni Roads. (ASBLFL.)

DAM GATE. The water level of the lake was controlled by opening and closing this old gate valve, which is no longer used. In the late fall, the gate was opened to drop the water level and keep the lake clean. In the spring and summer, the level was kept high so that town residents could enjoy swimming, fishing, and boating. (Courtesy John Allen.)

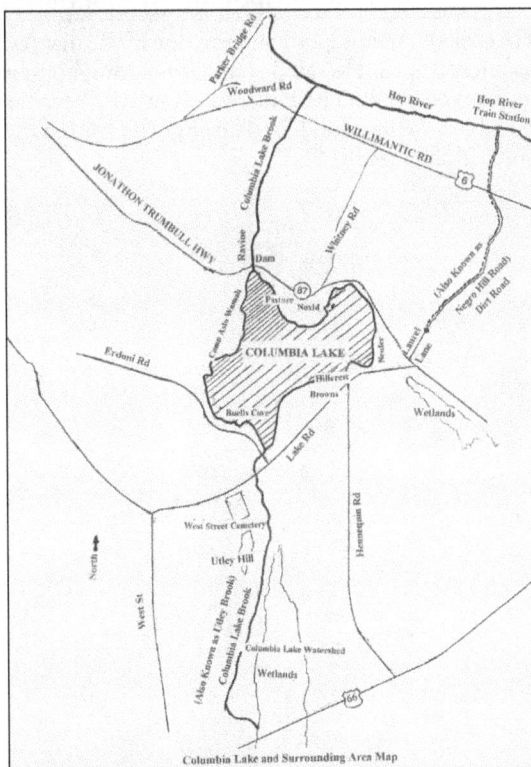

LAUREL LANE. After the turn of the 20th century, several businessmen bought or rented property around the lake, as their families sought refuge from the hot summers in the cities. Trains from Hartford and Willimantic stopped at the Hop River Station (see page 41). Visitors walked to the lake along a road now called Laurel Lane, shown on the map. (Courtesy John Allen.)

73

A. W. NORDLAND'S RESIDENCE. COLUMBIA, CONN.

HILLCREST. August Nordland was one of the first residents to predict the success of Columbia Lake as a resort area. He ran a summer boardinghouse called the Hillcrest, which rented out rooms and served meals. The Hillcrest eventually became the Loughrey home, and it was subsequently bought by William and Pat Murphy, who started the Columbia Canoe Club. The town now owns the building. (ASBLFL.)

The Group in the Pasture   Columbia, Conn.

NELLIE EDITH SAWYER. A visitor to Columbia in her childhood, Nellie Edith Sawyer, who was born in 1856, became an artist who specialized in miniatures. She opened a gallery in New York City. She and her sister purchased lakefront property from William Lyman in 1905 for $100. The compound of five cottages she built was known as the Pasture, and her home was named Afterthought. (ASBLFL.)

JOSEPHINE LAUTER GREER. Born in 1891, Greer was one of the most colorful and captivating personalities on Columbia Lake. She threw many parties at her home. Shown in this photograph are several of her friends. The famous actor Joe E. Brown is third from the left, and Greer is at far right. (ASBLFL.)

RED HOT MAMA. Although married, Josephine Greer traveled the vaudeville circuit and performed on stage from 1920 to 1937. She was accompanied on the piano by Georgia Sands. She often sang with Sophie Tucker and was her understudy in the Broadway production of *Last of the Red Hot Mamas*. She also played opposite Errol Flynn in a Broadway show called *Fiorta*. (ASBLFL.)

PHILLIP AND JOSEPHINE LAUTER. Phillip Lauter owned the Electro-Motive Company, the largest producer of mica capacitors in the world. When he died in 1945, Josephine became president. In 1972, the company was sold, and shortly thereafter, in 1975, it went bankrupt. (ASBLFL.)

JESSE GREER. Josephine remarried in 1948, to Jesse Greer, who was in the entertainment business. Greer wrote over 200 songs during his career. Some of his hit songs were "Just You Just Me," "Kitty from Kansas," "Marianne," and "Blessed Event." He played the piano, and often accompanied Josephine in her singing engagements. (ASBLFL.)

NOXID, C. 1940. Fannie Dixon Welch was another popular and notable person who lived on the lake. She built a beautiful home called Noxid ("Dixon" spelled backwards) on the lake and held social and political parties there. Many politicians, dignitaries, and important people from the Connecticut Democratic Party met there. Franklin and Eleanor Roosevelt visited her home several times, and FDR held at least one fireside chat there. Welch died in 1947. (CHS.)

JUNE NORCROSS. Another interesting resident of Columbia Lake was June Norcross. An illustrator, she started her own business designing and selling greeting and holiday cards. Her business thrived. One of her beautiful Christmas cards is shown here. (CHS.)

CORNET BAND. Early lake residents were entertained on summer weekends by the Columbia Cornet Band. Other bands entertained during the summer, including the Foster Band, which generally played at the Nuhfer property, on which was set up a large wooden bandstand stage. In the later 1920s, the Albert Lyman's school of music band performed. Some residents listened to the music from their boats, anchored near the concert area. (ASBLFL.)

FOSTER BAND. The Foster Band entertained during the long summer weekends. Concerts were held on the Nuhfer property, which at the time was a public swimming area with bathhouses, boat rentals, and a snack bar. (ASBLFL.)

HOO HOO CLUB AT COLUMBIA RESERVOIR, C. 1909. Columbia was a desirable camping destination in the summer. One of the groups that camped there was the Hoo Hoo Club, a local lumber industry organization. Note the old wooden chairs. (CHS.)

PICNIC AT CHESTNUT POINT, C. 1889. Ladies and men dressed in their finery are seen picnicking at the reservoir. Shown are, from left to right, Julia Avery, unidentified, Grace Sanger, unidentified, Edward Peel, Lucy Sawyer, unidentified, Addie Morgan, unidentified, Annie Hutchins, Lizzie Brown, George Sawyer, Rhoda Townsend, and Nellie Sawyer. (CHS.)

LAKESIDE BEACH, C. 1930. Refreshments were served at this lakeside store. Ice cream, soda, candy, and food were available to the summertime beach crowd. Note the public beach and diving platform. (ASBLFL.)

CAMP ASTO WAMAH, C. 1940. Many Columbia and out-of-town youngsters attended this summer camp. Here, boys are getting lessons on handling canoes and boats. Boaters on the lake can usually observe the youngsters in camp having a great time. (Courtesy N. Mclean.)

CAMP ASTO WAMAH SWIMMING PROGRAM. A large number of parents watch their children perform precision swimming programs in Columbia Lake. Swimming lessons were given in the morning, and the afternoons were devoted to "free swim periods." Campers were encouraged to help each other in order to develop a spirit of closeness and friendship. The camp's theme is "Remember the Other Fellow." (Courtesy N. Mclean.)

CAMP ASTO WAMAH CRAFTERS. These young ladies learn a variety of crafts at camp. They are all deeply engrossed in their projects and cannot wait to show their newly acquired skills to their parents. (Courtesy N. Mclean.)

AMPHIBIOUS PLANE. In Columbia Lake's early years, this type of aircraft was allowed to land and take off on the water. In 1948, a seaplane crashed on the lake, and the passenger was killed. A Columbia resident, Guy Beck, was able to rescue the pilot. (ASBLFL.)

C.R.C. AQUACADE 1948

AQUACADE. Every summer, the Columbia Recreation Council sponsored a large aquatic event at the lake. The Aquacade consisted of young women performing synchronized swimming programs. Large crowds of parents and friends gathered for the event. Note the old wooden dock. (ASBLFL.)

WINTER FUN, C. 1950. Junie Bell Squier and Raymond Squier skate on their ice pond near their home, now called the Landmark, located at the junction of Routes 87 and 66. (ASBLFL.)

COLUMBIA LAKE SAILING CLUB HOLDS RACES ON SUMMER SUNDAYS FOR SEASON AWARDS

SAILING CLUB. Sailing on Columbia Lake was in full swing as early as the 1930s. A sailing club was established not long after the Lake Association was formed in 1935. Sunday races are still common throughout the summer. Shown here are a Lightning-class sailboat and, in the background, a fleet of Sunfish. (ASBLFL.)

Six

MAKING THE
RULES AND REGULATIONS

The Town of Columbia was once the northern territory of Lebanon. William Clarke, Josiah Dewey, and Thomas Buckingham purchased this entire region from the Mohegan Indians; Abimeleck, and Oweneco, in 1699 and 1700. At this time, a church was organized and a minister selected. The church ran town politics, and only church members could vote. Soon after 1716, a second ecclesiastical society in the northern end of town called Lebanon Crank was established due to the remoteness of these parishioners from the main church. For almost 100 years, Lebanon Crank flourished under the new church leadership. In 1803, Lebanon Crank applied for incorporation of a new town to be called Columbia. It was granted in 1804. A selectman form of government was established, and that same year, Columbia's boundaries were established and voters elected town officials. They included five selectmen, tax collectors, a key keeper, a fencing inspector, and a chimney checker. In 1835, a Town House was built near the Old Yard Burying Ground. In addition to holding town meetings there, it was used for religious meetings, lectures, and concerts. In 1900, Mary Yeomans financed a new building, named in honor of her husband. It was for town administration use, including use by private organizations such as the Grange. Yeomans Hall burned down in 1940, and a new town hall was built. It is still in use.

There have been many changes in town politics and commercial enterprises since the beginning. The population has increased from 834, at the town's founding in 1804, to 5,370 in 2012. New businesses have been established along the Route 6 and Route 66 corridors, and large conservation and recreation areas have been set aside for use by town residents. Until 1960, Republicans dominated Columbia's elections; by 1970, Democrats were dominant. Today, the majority of voters are unaffiliated. Many changes have occurred over the years, but the town's character and beauty still remain. The rural, open atmosphere and the area's many historic buildings have been retained for the enjoyment of the residents of this peaceful community.

ADELLA URBAN. Columbia politics began in humble circumstances, with Freeman meetings in the Congregational Church. The first town hall was built in 1835, and subsequent meeting halls were constructed in 1900 and 1940. Highly popular, long-term town selectmen included Stephen Hosmer, Clair Robinson, Joseph Szegda, and Adella Urban. Here, Adella Urban (far right), a first selectman for 18 years, marches in Columbia's Fourth of July Parade. (ASBLFL.)

DECLARATION OF INDEPENDENCE FLOAT. Columbia residents have consistently maintained an interest in the nation's founding and political processes. This float, in a 1950s Fourth of July Parade, depicts the signing of the Declaration of Independence by Benjamin Franklin. The document, which proclaimed the colonies independent states, was adopted by the Continental Congress on July 4, 1776. The day has been celebrated with a parade in Columbia since the early 1900s. (ASBLFL.)

CONSTITUTION PIN OAK. A constitutional convention updated the Connecticut state constitution in Hartford in 1902. A pin oak was presented to each of the 168 state participants. This one, planted in front of the town hall, survived 95 years. Of the 74 that did survive, the average circumference was 9 feet, 10 inches, and the average height was 82 feet. (ASBLFL.)

DEMISE OF THE CONSTITUTION OAK. In the early spring of 1997, the Constitution Oak was found to be diseased. It was eventually cut down. Note the extremely large diameter of the trunk. Several people obtained wood from the tree and made tables and other furniture from it. A prime example of a table made from this tree can be found at The Meeting Place. (ASBLFL.)

ORIGINAL YEOMANS HALL. Mary B. Yeomans had this structure built in 1900 for the "free use by the Town and any of the organizations in town, secret or otherwise." However, stipulations were made that no drinking or dancing would be allowed. (ASBLFL.)

FIRE. Yeomans Hall was used as a meeting place for Columbia's town government for 40 years. In 1940, it was damaged in a spectacular fire, which swept from the basement to the upper hall and roof, where it was fanned by strong winds. The fire may have been caused by hot coals in an ash box in the basement or by faulty wiring. (ASBLFL.)

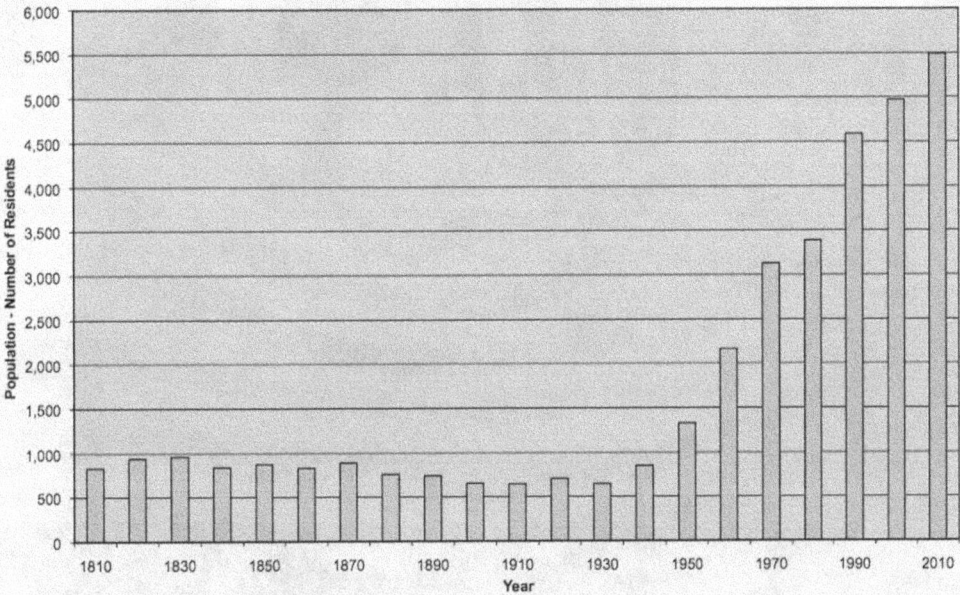

Columbia Population Trends

COLUMBIA'S POPULATION GROWTH. Significant population contraction occurred between 1830 and 1900 due to western migration and the attraction of urban centers with more job opportunities. Growth occurred after 1950 as servicemen returned home, new highways were built, and Columbia became part of the greater Hartford commuting area. Columbia's population trends are shown in this graph. (Courtesy John Allen.)

NEW TOWN HALL. After the fire, the old Yeomans Hall was torn down and replaced in 1941 by a one-and-a-half-story wooden building. Built at a cost of $22,000, the structure retained the name of the original benefactor, Mary B. Yeomans. In 1972, a $60,000 annex for administration offices was built, and in October 2011, it was dedicated to the memory of First Selectman Adella G. Urban. (ASBLFL.)

NEW FLAG DEDICATION, C. 1970. Two Boy Scouts and Columbia political leaders raise a new flag in front of Town Hall. Shown from left to right are two unidentified Boy Scouts, Robert Baldwin, Robert Steele, Howard Bates, and Joseph Szegda. (ASBLFL.)

COLUMBIA REPUBLICAN POLITICIANS, C. 1930. The three well-known Republican town officials shown here from left to right are town clerk Hubert Collins, First Selectman Clair Robinson, and Probate Judge Clayton Hunt. From the early years and into the 1960s, the town was generally Republican. Elections have favored Democrats from the 1960s to the present day. This coincides with the large increase in population during this time. (CHS.)

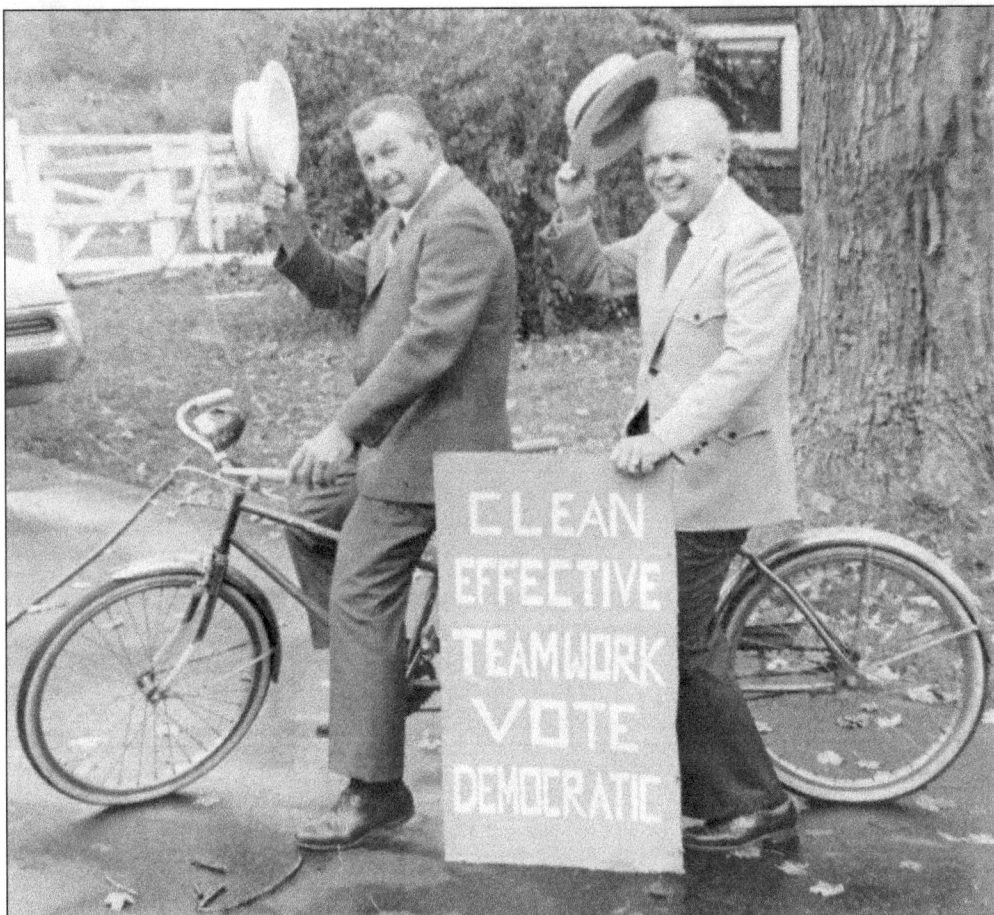

SELECTMAN ELECTION. Joseph Szegda (left) and Thomas O'Brien, Democratic town leaders, are seen tipping their hats on a bicycle made for two as they bid for a spot on the board of selectmen in the campaign of 1960. (ASBLFL.)

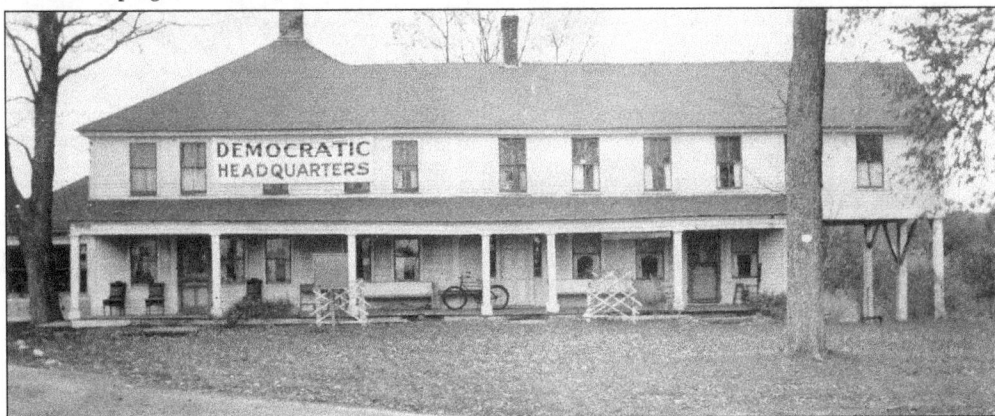

DEMOCRATIC HEADQUARTERS. The Landmark was the political headquarters for the Democrats in the 1960 elections. This building has had many uses through the years, including as an early tavern and stagecoach station, restaurant, drugstore, and commercial office building. In the wake of several strange occurrences, local citizens claimed that the building was haunted. (ASBLFL.)

COLUMBIA VOLUNTEER FIRE DEPARTMENT. The idea of a fire department in Columbia was presented at a meeting in October 1946. A year later, the Columbia Volunteer Fire Department (CVFD) was organized and incorporated at a meeting in Yeomans Hall on April 23, 1947. The first firehouse was erected that year with volunteer labor and land donated by Horace Porter. (ASBLFL.)

COLUMBIA VOLUNTEER FIREFIGHTERS. Early members of the CVFD pose in front of department vehicles. Shown are, from left to right, (first row) Walter Card, Richard Davis Sr., Ward Rosebrooks, Richard Davis Jr., Francis Lyman, Jack Card, Guy Beck, and Raymond Lyman; (second row) Harold Evans, Herbert Englert Jr., Herbert Englert Sr., and Boyd Tuttle, who identified these early members. There are currently over 100 members on the roster. (ASBLFL.)

EARLY POST OFFICE. Early post offices were often set up in private homes. Later, they were installed in stores, where the public more frequently visited. Finally, dedicated post offices were established, with mail delivery as the primary function. Lester Cooper built this post office in 1959 and leased it to the federal government. (ASBLFL.)

TOWN SIGNS. This little girl points to destinations near and far from the Columbia town center. This area is known to many as the crossroads of eastern Connecticut. The building in the background is the Landmark. Route 87 was not paved until the late 1920s. (Courtesy Squier Collection, ASBLFL.)

DEMOCRATIC WOMEN'S FLOAT, C. 1964. The Columbia Democratic and Republican parties had floats in the popular Fourth of July Parade. Many state and local officials also participated, marching or riding in convertibles and waving to and greeting constituents. The banner of the float shown here carries the famous Kennedy quote "Ask not what your country can do for you. Ask what you can do for your country." Parents and children alike sit at the side of Route 87 to watch the parade. The children are hopeful that candy may be thrown their way by some of the participants. Politicians still participate in this traditional parade. (ASBLFL.)

Seven

THE MEN AND WOMEN WHO WON AND KEPT OUR FREEDOM

Throughout the history of this great country, Columbia men and women have proudly served in the military. In frontier settlements, all able-bodied men were required to train for military action. Protection of family, homes, food, and livestock from hostile Indians required an alert response from all residents. When the Revolutionary War began, Lebanon Crank's contributions in men and material for the war effort were invaluable. Over two dozen local men fought in the Revolutionary War, and 21 are buried here. The Crank was a stop on the road to victory when Rochambeau's troops marched through town on their way to Yorktown. French regiments included the Bourbonnais, Soissonais, Royal Deux-Ponts, and Saintonge, and troops from 17 other countries signed on to fight for American ideals. It was an awe-inspiring sight: young soldiers, many of whom were French noblemen, wearing brilliant white coats and tight-fitting pants, their bright tricorn hats shading weary faces, and the bayonets of their muskets casting reflections from the sun's glistening rays. The young and the old brought food to the men, and a lass's kiss expressed the town's thanks. The sounds of the march were like music to residents' ears. This was a parade headed to war.

Columbia's list of war veterans include 17 from the Civil War, 18 from World War I, 121 from World War II, and approximately 30 each from the Korean conflict and the Vietnam War. Many Columbia men and women volunteered in other capacities to help during World War II. Duties included observation of aircraft, selling war bonds, collecting newspapers and scrap metals, selective service duties, and rationing boards. Two women's groups, the British War Relief Group and the Columbia Older Girls Society (COGS), were especially helpful to the war efforts. It is with great pride that we pay homage in this chapter to all of those Columbia men and women who served our country with honor, courage, and dignity.

REV. THOMAS BROCKWAY GRAVESTONE. Prior to the war, Reverend Brockway (page 7) was espousing the colonial revolutionary cause and decrying British rule in his sermons to his parishioners. An adamant patriot, he served as a chaplain in Col. Samuel Selden's regiment in the Connecticut militia in 1776. His gravestone can be found in the Old Yard Burying Ground. (Courtesy John Allen.)

REVOLUTIONARY WAR FRENCH BAYONET. During the Revolutionary War, French troops were bivouacked on the town green in Lebanon and Columbia. Many made frequent stops at the Lebanon Crank Inn to buy supplies and imbibe a few drinks. Marshall Squier, who owned the inn in the 1950s, found a musket hidden in an attic wall. This French 1760s Charleville rifle bayonet was found in Columbia by John Allen. (Courtesy John Allen.)

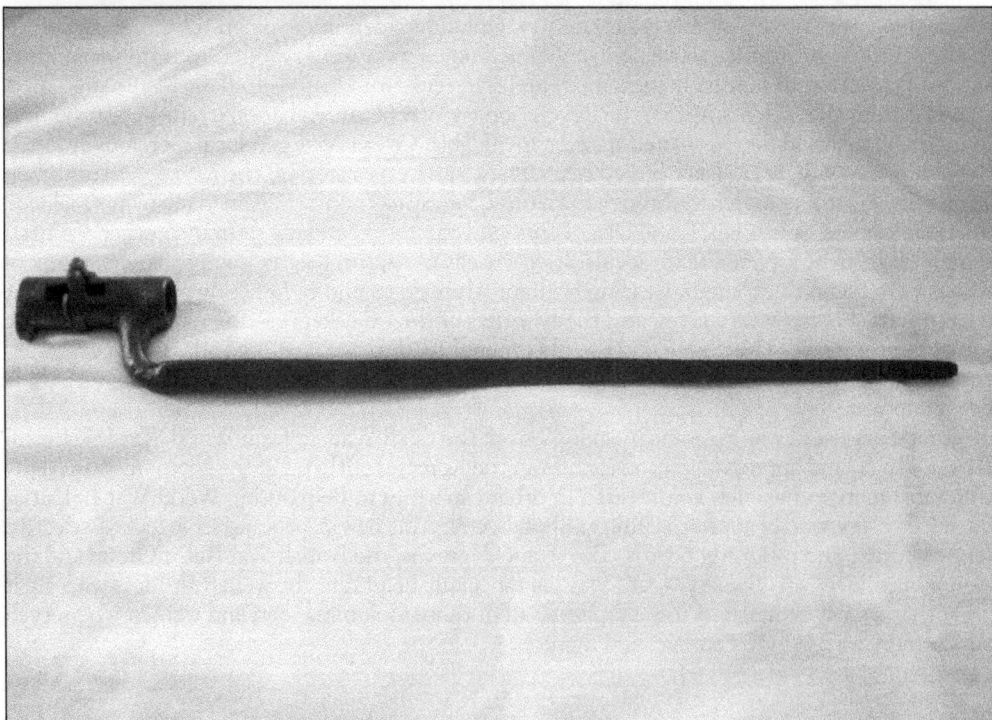

BRITISH WAR RELIEF GROUP.

A group of 20 women from Columbia knitted, sewed, and made clothing and garments for English victims of German bombing raids before the United States entered World War II. Items included 500 wool quilts and afghans, 600 wool garments, and many soft toys for children. Shown is a page of the group's final report, with a note from the British embassy. (ASBLFL.)

REPORT OF THE BRITISH WAR RELIEF GROUP

Miss Edith Sawyer, Miss Katherine Ink and Miss Anne Dix. One summer resident, Miss Katherine Christhilf, gave her time for the five summers. Last, but not least, is Mrs. Marshall Squier, who saw to it that we had hot coffee every Thursday noon for five years.

Although only two of the group were British born, nevertheless all the members felt a special bond of kinship and sympathy with the English people in their time of trouble and were glad to be able to express that feeling for them through this work.

This "kinship" is proved by the following letter.

British Embassy

Washington, 8, D. C.

His Majesty's Ambassador presents his compliments to Miss Anne Dix and has the honour to inform her that The King has been pleased to award her His Majesty's Medal for Service in the Cause of Freedom.

Lord Inverchapel would like to offer his personal congratulations on this well merited award.

July 9th, 1946.

TO

Mrs. Cora Hutchins

AS the activities of THE BRITISH WAR RELIEF SOCIETY OF AMERICA draw to a close, we wish to add to the sentiments of gratitude for American generosity from the people of Great Britain already voiced by Prime Minister Churchill and British Ambassador the Earl of Halifax, our expression of heartfelt appreciation for your continued and splendid cooperation.

You have demonstrated in a most practical manner that you share the sentiment recently expressed publicly in London by General Eisenhower:

"One of the passions of my life is to promote real and practical cooperation among your people and ours."

PRESIDENT

COMMITTEE CHAIRMAN

LETTER OF APPRECIATION. The British War Relief Group received His Majesty's Medal for Service in the Cause of Freedom from the King's ambassador. The letter was addressed to Cora Hutchins, leader of the Columbia group. The items made and sent by the organization raised the spirits of the British people and signaled that American help was close at hand. (ASBLFL.)

THE COGWHEEL

Edited by the COGS   December

This is your Christmas edition of the Cogwheel and here's hoping most of you will receive it before December 25. This year more than ever before, Christmas will have a special meaning for us. We will learn to value more highly the little things that make our American way of living so dear to us. Christmas is one of the American institutions we are fighting to maintain. Although most of you will not be here this year, everyone back home will be thinking of you and missing every one of you. Let us pray that by another year, peace and good will will be well on the way.

It seems Luke Robinson was convalescing from his broken ankle when they brought a fellow with a broken toe in and put him in the next bed. Well, of course the two got to talking, and it developed that the new boy had an aunt who lives in Columbia. Yes, he is none other than Bob Failor, nephew of Lisa Dix, a well known local resident. We are glad you have company, Luke, and here's hoping you will soon be back to normal.

George Redford, uncle of Sgt. George Peters, had just returned from a visit with his nephew in Laredo, Texas. They had a wonderful time visiting with each other and spent Thanksgiving together.

We received your card in good order, Sgt. Bernard Meyerson. We understand you are doing a swell job as an instructor in aerial gunnery-- keep up the good work!

We hear that Eleanor Jackson way down in Australia has her room filled with Orchids every day. That's the Soldiers' way of showing their appreciation. You're doing a important job Eleanor, and here's wishing you all the best of luck.

We received your letter of October 25, Cpl. Bob Church and were glad to hear you enjoyed your furlough. You bet we can give you Spencer Kacht's address. Its P.F.C. Spencer Kacht 31122968, Hp. Co. 10, P of E, A.P.O. 758, c/o Postmaster, New York, N.Y.

COGS would like to take this opportunity to express their gratitude and appreciation to Mr. Rowland for the use of his mimeograph and his help in printing this paper each month. Without his assistance, the Cogwheel would not be possible.

We received your letter P.F.C. Louis Axelrod. No, the crows aren't fooling us any longer, as the Observation post is being operated only on the second Wednesday of each month now.

Thanks for sending us your P.O. address, Charlie Perkins! It really is a big help. Now you will undoubtedly receive your Cogwheel instead of its being returned to us. Also the best of luck to you.

Christmas will be observed in Columbia this year in the traditional manner. There will be Christmas music and a Christmas sermon in Church, December 19. The Sunday School program including Santa Claus as usual, will be that afternoon. A special evening service will be held December 26 in the Church including appropriate music and a narative by Mrs. Madeline Mitchell of Columbia. The Girl Scouts are planning to sing carols from house to house on Christmas Eve.

That letter of yours was definitely worth waiting for, P.F.C. Len German. We enjoyed your account of your adventures in England and we also were glad to get such a nice long letter. Wish we could see some of those castles and mansions you described, but since letters are as close as we can get to these things, thanks a lot for writing.

In some ways, it hardly seems possible that another December 7 has come and gone marking the second anniversary of our entry into this mighty conflict. We have worked very hard for what we have accomplished, and we will put even more effort into the months to come. Victory must be ahead of us, and let us hope it will be soon.

(Over)

COGS. Six Columbia women started an organization called the Columbia Older Girls Society (COGS) at the beginning of World War II. They published a newsletter, the COGWHEEL, a sample of which is shown here. The publication, sent to all Columbia servicemen and servicewomen, provided local news, veteran updates, and war news. (ASBLFL.)

SERVICEMAN'S LETTER. World War II servicemen and servicewomen were thrilled to receive the COGWHEEL. Soldiers' letters describing their well-being and experiences abroad supplied the COGS ladies with material for the newsletter. Every letter written to the society expressed the soldiers' appreciation for receiving this publication, which gave them a taste of home and of their life in Columbia. They were anxious to get news about friends, promotions, duties, and locations. (ASBLFL.)

COGS Honor Roll Dedication. On March 26, 1944, the COGS dedicated an honor roll of all veterans of World War II to the Town of Columbia. Dances were held to support the project. The COGS ladies posing with veteran sailor Gus Naumec (center) are, from left to right, Jane Lyman McKeon, Olive Tuttle Shea, Jean Isham Peters, Kaye Sharpe Anderson, Shirley Trythall Kurcinik, and Carol Lyman Ladd. (ASBLFL.)

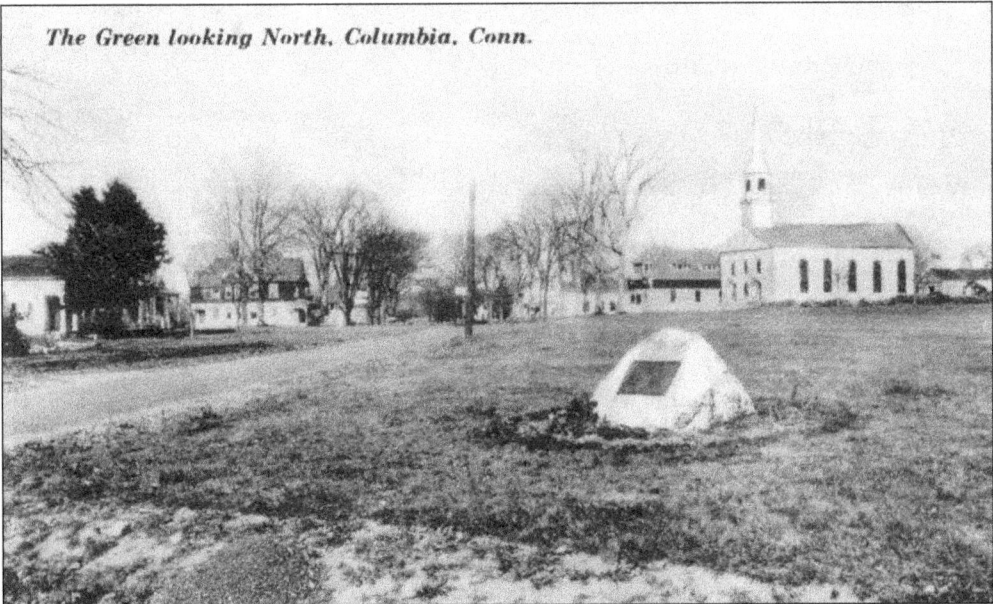

The Green looking North, Columbia, Conn.

World War I Memorial. The bronze plaque attached to the boulder was dedicated by the town to all servicemen who served in World War I. It is located on the town green. Of the 18 men who served, two were killed: Cyrus Hilton and Stanley Hunt. (ASBLFL.)

MEMORIAL AND FLAGPOLE. This memorial on the town green, donated by the Lions Club, honors all veterans of World War II. The flag and memorial are lighted at night, a tribute to all of those from Columbia who served the country. (ASBLFL.)

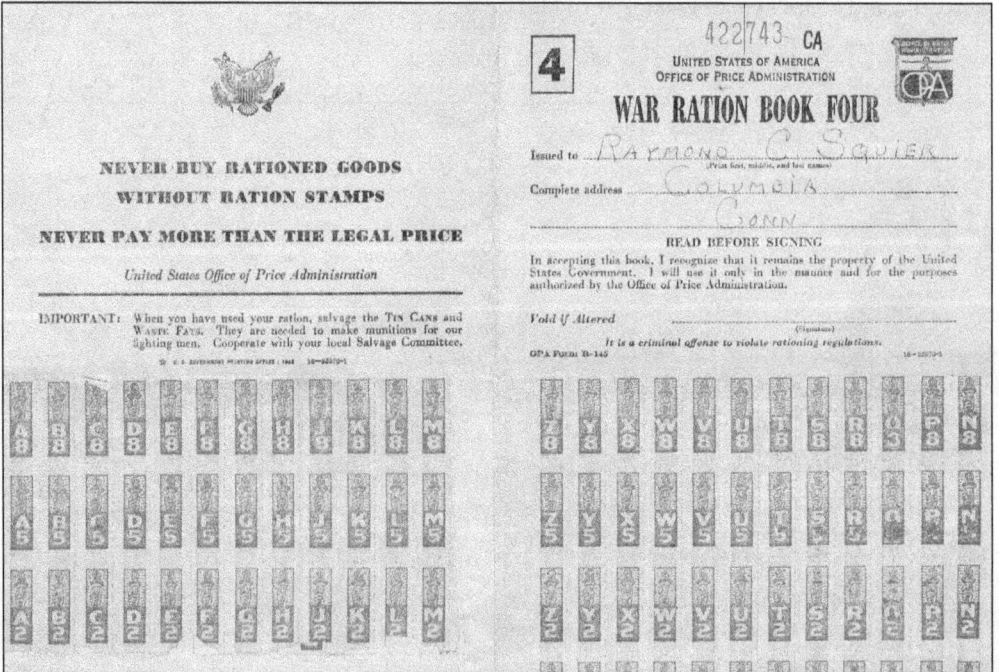

CIVILIAN VOLUNTEERS. Those who did not serve in the military during World War II volunteered for a wide variety of tasks in the war effort. Volunteers served on the selective service and rationing boards, acted as air raid wardens, sold war bonds, collected scrap metal and paper, and made surgical dressings. Shown here is a typical war ration stamp book. (ASBLFL.)

SCRAP METAL DRIVE, C. 1942.
Wilberforce T. Little contributes his
share of scrap metal to the war effort.
Any type of metal was acceptable,
even old horseshoes. The scrap
iron was converted into machinery
employed to win the war. (ASBLFL.)

NAVAL GUNNER. Wilberforce T.
Little, age 92, wears his World
War I dress uniform. He served as
a gunner in the Navy from 1917
to 1921. He was also in the Naval
Reserve for four years. (ASBLFL.)

OBSERVATION TOWER, c. 1942. This small building on Route 66, known as Freeman No. 52, was used as a lookout for enemy aircraft during World War II. The site is on Post Hill, which, at an elevation of 775 feet above sea level, is one of the highest points in eastern Connecticut. Shown at the door to the observation tower are Fred Lambert (left), Adolph German (center), and Don Woodward. (Courtesy Belle Robinson.)

RESTORED TOWER. The Aircraft Tower on Post Hill (also known as Skyline Farm) in Columbia was moved to the town of Hebron, where it was restored. The Hebron Historic Commission led the restoration project. The tower, one of 14,000 that were manned 24 hours a day, every day during 1942, is thought to be the only one still in existence. It is now located on Hebron's town hall green. (Courtesy John Allen.)

CORP. CHARLES GRANT. Corporal Grant served in the Army in 1958 and 1959 as a member of A Battery, 2nd Howitzer Battalion, 8th Artillery. Grant (first row, second from right) poses with his artillery school unit. He served in Korea one half-mile from the demilitarized zone. (Courtesy Charles Grant.)

T.SGT. EDWARD WENDUS. Technical Sergeant Wendus served in the Army from early 1943 to December 1945 in the 2nd Armored Division, 66th Regiment, Company A. He was a tank driver and gunner, and is shown here on his M24 tank. He landed on Omaha Beach on D-Day + 2, and was awarded five major battle stars, a presidential citation, and a Bronze Star. (Courtesy Edward Wendus.)

MERTON WOLFF. Wolff served as a surgical technician in the Army Medical Corps, 71st Area Service Unit, from August 1945 to November 1946. He is shown relaxing on the side steps of the barracks of the regional station hospital in Fort Belvoir, Virginia. (Courtesy Merton Wolff.)

RUSSELL INZINGA. Joining the Merchant Marines in October 1943, Inzinga served aboard the ship *Edward B. Alexander* as a steward during the entire war. On his first trip to Scotland, German aircraft attacked the ship, which was carrying 12,000 troops. One boat in the convoy was sunk. Inzinga (left) is shown on board the ship with his friend Michael Reikite. (Courtesy Russell Inzinga.)

COLUMBIA PARADE, C. 1960s. Veterans riding on a REO truck display a machine gun, M1 rifles, and a bazooka. Among the veterans are Phillip Isham (on the roof, straddling the machine gun) and Emil Sadlon (in the back, standing with the flag). (ASBLFL.)

BELLE ROBINSON. Not all of the war effort involved fighting. Belle Robinson (left) and Jean Copp (right) worked for the Federal Bureau of Investigation as a Morse code radio operator during World War II. She made trips to New Haven, Connecticut; Portland, Oregon; San Francisco, California; and Washington, DC, where she monitored clandestine enemy communications. (Courtesy Belle Robinson.)

BARBERING SKILLS. Russell Inzinga (center) practices his barbering skills on several WACs with shampoo and hair sets aboard the ship *Edmund B. Alexander*. The men were on their way to France during World War II. The women seemed pleased to be so accommodated and rather surprised to find this service aboard ship. (Courtesy Russell Inzinga.)

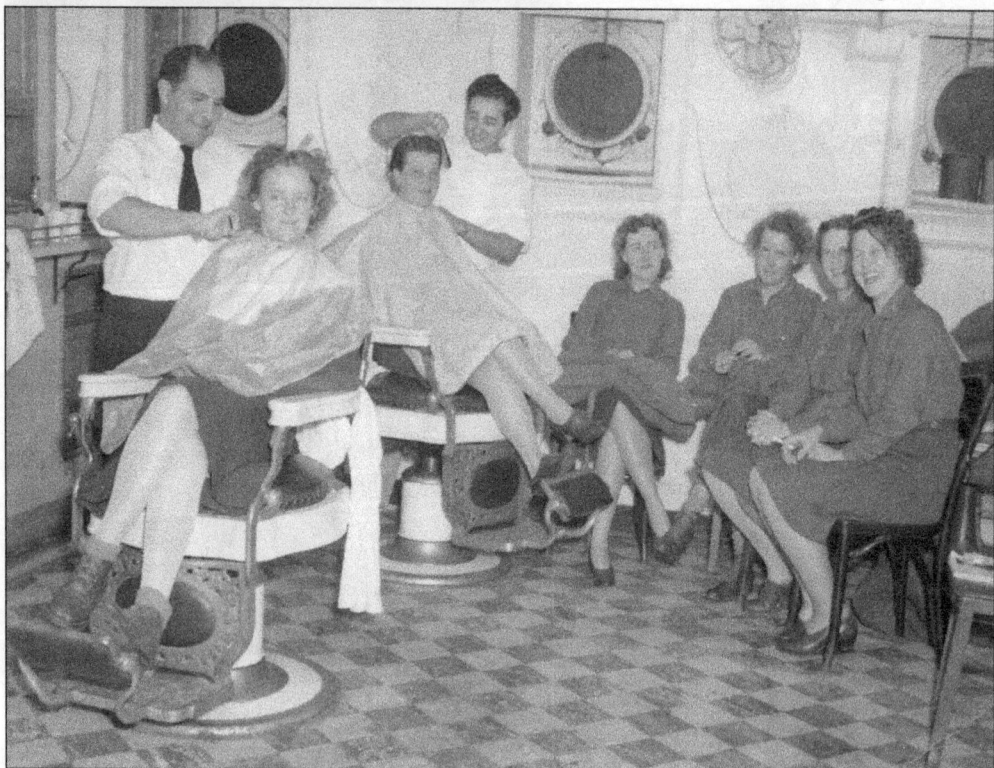

Eight

ORGANIZED SPORTS AND SOCIAL ACTIVITIES

One of the most popular sports in Columbia, and indeed in the nation today, is baseball. It has been played in town since close to its beginnings in the 1870s. Early baseball games in Columbia were played on the town green. Home plate was located near Collins Garage, and center field was toward the Congregational Church. Dr. Julian LaPierre laid out the field and organized Columbia's first team. Other nearby towns formed teams, organized leagues, and set up inter-town schedules. Families made picnic lunches, spread blankets on the grass, and enjoyed the games—much the same as it is done today. Another popular sporting activity was canoe and kayak racing. The Columbia Canoe Club was started by Pat Murphy in 1961. It went on to achieve national and worldwide recognition. The club hosted several national events on Columbia Lake. Other popular sports activities have included sailing, archery, and skiing. The Columbia Recreation Council was organized in 1946 and offered many programs. There were dances for teenagers and young adults, several aquatic activities including swimming lessons and a girls' synchronized swimming group called the Aquacades, beauty contests, gymnastics, basketball, hockey, and bowling. Adult programs included art classes, swimming lessons, and hobby shows. The council also sponsored a Memorial Day service, a Fourth of July parade, and a Christmas carol sing, the latter two of which are now part of the Lions Club programs.

DR. JULIAN LAPIERRE. LaPierre laid out the first baseball diamond on the Columbia town green in the 1870s. He also organized the first baseball team in Columbia, managed it, and even acted as umpire. A careful examination of the photograph on pages 20 and 21 shows early baseball players on the green. In one game, Herb Post hit a ball over the church roof. (CHS.)

COLUMBIA'S 1916 BASEBALL TEAM. Baseball has been a tradition in Columbia since after the Civil War. Gloves were not used, and fielders could get a batter out by either catching a ball on the fly or the first bounce. The 1916 team members pictured are, from left to right, (first row) Raymond Squier, Llewelyn Latham, and Horace Little; (second row) Roland Cobb, Phillip Isham, Robert Cobb, William Friedrich, Herbert Collins, and Edward La Bonte. (CHS.)

COLUMBIA CRANKS, 2004. This old-time baseball team was formed during Columbia's bicentennial. Team members are, from left to right, (first row) Christopher DelMastro and Jason DelMastro; (second row) Ronald Wikholm, Keith Curry, William McConaughy, Steven Everette, and Brian Wade; (third row) Alan Wade, Manager George Skinner, William Bright, Scott Vezina, Frank Giovannini, Peter Ganci, and umpire David Grzytch. (ASBLFL.)

COLUMBIA BASEBALL FIELDS. After the town center was built up and baseball could no longer be played there, several fields were established around town. Firemen's Field, Katzman's Corner Field, and Hutchins' Field were a few. In 1972, the town built the Recreation Park and established three baseball fields. Recreation Council officials pose with a sign pointing the way to the new fields. (ASBLFL.)

DONKEY BASEBALL, C. 1959. In many cases, baseball games were played strictly for fun and entertainment. Here, two ladies, Nancy Nuhfer (left) and Velva Lennox, prepare donkeys for a game against the men. At times, the donkeys were very cantankerous; controlling them was more of a challenge than playing the game. (CHS.)

JUNIOR DIVISION BASEBALL CHAMPS. Baseball in Columbia has been played at many age levels. These Columbia youth won the Junior Division Championship of 1953. The team members are, from left to right, (first row) Brian Sinder, Louis Sorrachi, Ronald Cobb, and Francis Baker; (second row) William Macht, John Wheaton, Enn Koiva, Leonard King, and Thomas Collins. (CHS.)

PAT MURPHY. Pat Murphy founded the Columbia Canoe Club in 1961. She spent eight to ten hours a day teaching paddling basics and the techniques of canoe and kayak racing to her students. Her standards were strict. Students would have to execute up to 500 paddle strokes while sitting at the dock before getting into their canoe or kayak. (ASBLFL.)

CANOE CLUB MEMBERS. The Columbia Canoe Club hosted several national races at Columbia Lake starting in 1964. Members of the club practice with Sterling Brightman (rear), Pat Murphy (in front of Sterling, to his right), and Mary Fletcher (in front of Sterling, to his left). The club won the President's Cup in Washington, DC, in 1963. (CHS.)

WORLD RECOGNITION.
Columbia Canoe Club
members Robert Fletcher
(left) and Dennis Murphy
are in their traveling suits,
getting ready to attend
the International Regatta
in Berlin, Germany. Both
represented the United States
in the 1966 International
Canoe Club Championships
in East Germany. (CHS.)

ARCHERY. Arthur Hall gives
an archery lesson to a young
lady. Hall introduced the
sport in Columbia in the
1950s. Lessons were initially
taught to archers at Dr. Ralph
Wolmer's yard on Lake Road
and later at Max Lessenger's
property at Mono Pond.
The club built a 25-target
course and a clubhouse on
the property. (ASBLFL.)

ARCHERY COMPETITION, C. 1958. Members of the Columbia Archery Club participated in many competitive matches. In this photograph, men, women, and youngsters receive trophies in their respective classes. In later years, Arthur Hall opened his own successful archery business. (ASBLFL.)

SKI CLUB MEMBER PROGRESS REPORT. The Columbia Recreation Council organized a ski club in the 1950s. It was quite active for many years. Each member of the ski club was required to qualify in several categories when learning to ski. The progression to expert slopes required proficiency in all categories. (ASBLFL.)

Order of Technique		
REQUIREMENTS	APPROVED	DATE
Use of poles		
Walking		
Kick turn		
Side step		
Herringbone		
Traverse-kick-turn		
Snow plow		
Snow plow turn		
Slow stem turn		
Fast stem turn		
Stem christie		
Schwingen		
Parallel christie		
Pure (stop) christie		
Slalom		
Jump turn		
Terrain jump		
Trail running		
O K for 4th class test		
O K for 3rd class test		
O K for 2nd class test		
Passed 4th class test		
Passed 3rd class test		
Passed 2nd class test		

SKI CLUB. The Columbia Recreation Council organized a variety of sporting activities in town. Members of the Columbia Ski Club ready for action are, from left to right, (first row) Caroline Petroquin, unidentified, Richard Young, unidentified, Betty Bernet, Nancy Nuhfer, Gwen Bronson, and Douglas Wolmer; (second row) Nancy Woodward, Wallace Lohr, Leona Wolmer, Richard Davis, Ralph Wolmer, Herbert Englert, Dean Tibbits, Victor Wolmer, Ernest Payne, and Wilber Fletcher. The ski area appears to be on top of Utley Hill, with Columbia Lake in the background. Note the openness of the area, with no homes nearby. The group consisted of younger boys and girls as well as adults. There were no ski lifts, so plenty of energy was required to get to the top. (ASBLFL.)

COLUMBIA RECREATION COUNCIL. The council was formed in 1946 to promote leisure-time activities for youth and adults. The first nine chairmen of the organization are, from left to right, (first row) Jack Card, Wilbur Fletcher, Eleanor Tuttle, and Ralph Wolmer; (second row) Charles Randall, Howard Thayer, Maurice Clark, Joseph Lusky, and Carl Gosline. (CHS.)

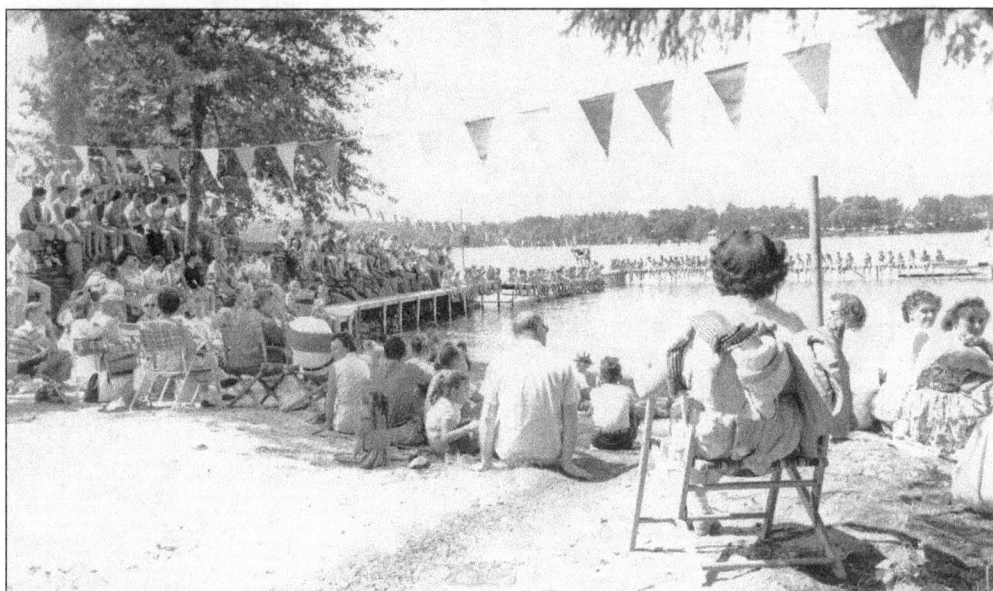

SWIMMING PERFORMANCE, C. 1957. Huge audiences attended the swimming performance programs at the town beach. Many spectators brought their beach chairs along to spend the afternoon watching the boys and girls display their newly acquired skills. Note the old wooden dock, a relic of the past, and children sitting along the dock waiting for their turn to impress their parents and friends. (ASBLFL.)

COLUMBIA AQUACADES. This group of synchronized precision swimmers performed at many Columbia Recreation Council summer programs at the lake. Shown are, from left to right, Joanne Gadoury, Sally Card, Dayna Thompson, Karen Hirn, Cheryl Berkowitz, Lee German, Karen Wolmer, Nancy Bartolan, Pamela Lusky, unidentified, and Andrea Stimpson. (ASBLFL.)

HAWAIIAN WATER BALLET. These Columbia ballet swimmers take time out to pose for a photograph. Pictured are, from left to right, (first row) Joanne Gadoury, unidentified, Pamela Lusky, unidentified, Judy Hills, Eileen Alexander, and Sally Hutchins; (second row) Dayna Thompson, Sally Card, Linda Collins, Patricia Murphy, Dianne Sanden, Donna Rosen, two unidentified, and Andrea Stimpson. (ASBLFL.)

116

CALENDAR GIRLS, C. 1950. These beautiful Columbia girls pose for a photograph. Shown are, from left to right, Nancy Nuhfer, Joanne Armstrong, Dorothy Jensen, Betty Burnett, Lillian Banner, Ann Hennricks, Claudia Ethridge, Betty Falk, Betty Trotter, Gwen Tibbits, June Squier, unidentified, Barbara Silverstein, Judy Jackson, Phyllis Silverstein, and Sheila Panos. (ASBLFL.)

SPRING FORMAL, C. 1950. The Columbia Recreation Council not only organized sporting events, but also sponsored a formal dance every spring. Here, young men display their fancy hats in a competitive rivalry. Perhaps the winner of this event got a chance to dance with his choice of young ladies. (ASBLFL.)

117

FORMAL DANCE. Young men and women in formal attire participate in the spring dance sponsored by the Columbia Recreation Council. Rock and roll, in its infancy in the early 1950s, was soon accepted and enjoyed by the young. (ASBLFL.)

HOBBY SHOW, C. 1949. Columbia residents display some of their many interesting and varied hobbies and collections at an exhibit sponsored by the Recreation Council. A young lady finds an interesting seat at the hobby show. She has many to choose from. (ASBLFL.)

Nine

FRATERNAL AND CIVIC ORGANIZATIONS

Charitable fraternal and civic organizations have provided social, economic, and political benefits to Columbia. The Masons were the first fraternal group to organize in Columbia, forming Lyon Lodge No. 105 in 1868. David Buell was the first master of the lodge, which had 37 charter members. They initially met in Bascom Hall at the Old Inn and later at the old Porter Store, near the center of town. The Masons founded and still support many charities, including 22 children's hospitals nationwide and facilities that care for the elderly. The Columbia Grange No. 131 was the second fraternal group in Columbia. Charles Reed was the first master of this group, which was chartered in 1892. The 35 charter members also met in Bascom Hall until 1900, and then in Yeomans Hall. The grange supported the farming community with educational programs and youth farming activities and was active in lobbying in Washington to promote agricultural interests. The Columbia Lions Club was founded in 1955 with 22 charter members. William S. Burnham was the first president. Meetings were held at the Ox Yoke Restaurant in Columbia and later at the Log Cabin Restaurant in Lebanon, where the club still meets today. The Lions Club, nationally recognized for its eye health-care programs, is also well known in Columbia for its numerous community projects. The Knights of Columbus Roman Catholic fraternal organization was chartered in Columbia as No. 6305 in 1974. There were 23 charter members. The organization met at St. Columba Church. The Knights support the pro-life Culture of Life charity and provide relief aid to victims of disasters. Other civic organizations covered in this chapter are the Boy Scouts, Girl Scouts, Columbia Historical Society, and Joshua's Trust Land Conservancy. Although several of the local fraternal organizations are no longer present in the town, the history and contributions of each are a gentle reminder of past contributions that are still felt today in many different ways.

SIXTH : ANNUAL

MASONIC : BALL.

: 1885 :

Eng by J.A.Lowell & L° Boston USA

LYON·LODGE NO. 105

A. F. AND A. M.

OF : COLUMBIA : CONN.

WILL : GIVE : A

GRAND : MASONIC

Calico : Dress : Ball

AT : BASCOM'S : HALL

WEDNESDAY : EVENING, : JAN. : 28.

: YOUR : COMPANY : WITH : LADIES : IS : SOLICITED :

MASONIC FRATERNAL ORGANIZATION. Columbia's Lyon Lodge No. 105 was chartered in 1868 with 37 members. David Buell was the first master. The group held square dances at the Old Inn ballroom, Bascom Hall. An 1885 square dance program called Calico Dance Card is seen here. Note the phrase "Your Company With Ladies is Solicited." The price of the dance and supper was $1.50. (ASBLFL.)

SECOND GRANGE MASTER. The second group to organize in town was Columbia Grange No. 131, chartered in 1892. Charles Reed was the first master of the Grange, which had 35 charter members. William A. Collins Jr. (pictured) was the second master. Programs included social interaction to provide a relief to farmers from the physical and mental demands of their occupation. (CHS.)

AMELIA FULLER, C. 1893. Fuller, shown here in her lovely dress, was the first secretary of Columbia Grange No. 131. Meetings of the Grange were held in the Old Inn until 1895, when the members decided to meet in the old Masonic Hall. The building, the former home of Myrtle Collins, no longer stands. (CHS.)

COLUMBIA GRANGE DRILL TEAM. These eight young Columbia ladies, Grange members, participate in a ceremony at Yeomans Hall. The dresses, hats, and shawls are part of the required attire. (ASBLFL.)

KNIGHTS OF COLUMBUS. The Knights of Columbus march in Columbia's Fourth of July Parade. The town's Knights of Columbus order, No. 6305, originated in October 1971 with 26 charter members. The organization met at St. Columba Church on Monday and Thursday nights. There are four other councils in the nearby towns of Hebron, East Hampton, Moodus, and Portland. (Courtesy Merton Wolff.)

PROGRAM

Call to Order and
Introduction of Toastmaster .... Maurice Alexander
Charter Night Chairman

Toastmaster of Evening .... Al Urbinati
Representative, Lions International

Song — "Star-Spangled Banner" .... The Assembly

Pledge of Allegiance .... The Assembly

Invocation .... Rev. Henry G. Wyman
Pastor, Congregational Church, Columbia

Lions Toast

DINNER

Songs .... The Assembly

Introduction of Guests and Visiting Clubs .... Toastmaster

Presentation of Charter .... Thomas E. Shackley
District Governor, Lions International

Acceptance of Charter .... William S. Burnham
President of Columbia Lions Club

Presentation of Gong and Gavel .... Philip Baker
Lebanon Lions

Presentation of Flag .... Charles Naylor
International Director

Address .... Philip H. Isham

Closing Song — "Till We Meet Again" .... The Assembly

Benediction .... Rev. Henry G. Wyman

DANCING

Menu

FRUIT CUP

BARBECUE CHICKEN

WHIPPED POTATOES   RELISHES

BREAD AND BUTTER

VEGETABLES

ROLLS AND BUTTER

BULK ICE CREAM AND COOKIES

COFFEE WITH CREAM

COLUMBIA LIONS CLUB. The Columbia Lions is perhaps the most recognized of all organizations in town because of its numerous community contributions. The club was organized in 1955 as an offshoot of the Willimantic Lions. An original program for a charter recognition celebration is shown, listing the newly elected officers, original charter members, board of directors, and the program for the evening. (Courtesy Columbia Lions Club.)

122

GOOD DEED. The first project of the Columbia Lions Club was its contribution of an audiometer (hearing evaluator) to the Horace W. Porter School. Posing with the device are, from left to right, (first row) unidentified, school board chairman Donald Tuttle, first president of the Columbia Lions William Burnham, and school principal George Patros; (second row) George Peters, Mrs. Paul Merrick, Walter Card, Mrs. George Peters, and Gene Dente. (Courtesy Columbia Lions Club.)

BEACH HOUSE PLAQUE. Another Lions Club project, initiated in 1957, involved the building of a new beach house on Columbia Lake to replace the obsolete structures. First Selectman Clair Robinson presents a plaque to commemorate the building. Pictured are, from left to right, Robinson, Selectman Phillip Isham, and Lions members George Smith and Prescott Hodges. (Courtesy Columbia Lions Club.)

MINSTREL SHOW REHEARSAL. John McVeigh, at the piano, practices a song with fellow Lions for the yearly minstrel show. Standing behind McVeigh are, from left to right, Kenneth Erickson, Gene Dente, Morris Alexander, Morris Kaplan, Charles Olson, and Howard Bates. (Courtesy Columbia Lions Club.)

LIONS LADIES NIGHT. It was not only the men who enjoyed the Lions programs. Here, several ladies dressed in costumes are enjoying an evening program at Yeomans Hall. Pictured are, from left to right, Judy Quimby, Sandra Lohr, Helen Laramie, Lorraine Lewis, and Betty Hill. All enjoyed an evening of dancing, laughter, and gourmet food. (Courtesy Columbia Lions Club.)

124

OTHER LIONS PROJECTS. The Columbia Lions Club has provided the town with many community amenities, including the town gazebo, the veterans memorial, and the Firemen's Field. In addition, the Lions co-sponsor the Fourth of July Parade. Shown here is a float from one of the earliest parades sponsored by the Lions. (ASBLFL.)

COLUMBIA BOY SCOUTS. Scouting in Columbia started in December 1942, when the Parent Teacher Organization accepted a charter for Boy Scout Troop 62. The first scoutmaster was Reginald Lewis, followed by E. Malcolm Stannard and Wilbur Fletcher. Shown at the COGS Honor Roll dedication are three Boy Scouts dressed in suits for the occasion, with Gus Naumec (center, in Navy uniform) and Guy Beck (far right). (Courtesy Merton Wolff.)

125

COLUMBIA GIRL SCOUTS. This Girl Scout flag ceremony at the Horace W. Porter School was in commemoration of Girl Scouts all over the world. Here, scouts are dressed in Brownie, Cadette, Junior, Mariner, and foreign nation uniforms. Note the Girl Scout trefoil logo on the table holding the globe, as well as the Girl Scout flag to the far right. (ASBLFL.)

BROWNIES IN PARADE, C. 1950. The first Girl Scout troop in Columbia was established in 1938, sponsored by the Ladies Aid Society. The troop leader was Leona M. Wolmer, with assistants Lois E. Clarke, Beula M. Collins, Jean L. Natsch, and Brownie Hopkins. Here, Brownies ride in a decorated 1950s Crosley station wagon in the Fourth of July Parade. (ASBLFL.)

COLUMBIA HISTORICAL SOCIETY. In 1966, the Horace W. Porter School Board of Education recommended the creation of a historical society. A committee was formed, and the society gathered 112 charter members. The first officers were Edith C. Haver (president), Donald R. Tuttle (vice president), Gladys Rice (secretary), and Philip H. Isham (treasurer). On September 14, 2012, past presidents Arlene Gray, Albert Gray, and Belle Robinson, as well as town historian De Ramm, were honored with Lifetime Achievement Awards for their many years of service in preserving and promoting Columbia's history. Belle Robinson and De Ramm are seen here receiving congratulations. (Courtesy John Allen.)

JOSHUA TRUST. The Joshua Trust, initiated in 1966, owns over 1,000 acres of preservation land. The 118-acre Utley Hill Preserve, Clarke House farmland, and Potter Meadow area in Columbia are part of the conservation land. Shown here on a tour of the Utley Hill area are longtime member Albert Gray (second from left) and his wife, Arlene Gray (fourth from left). (ASBLFL.)

Visit us at
arcadiapublishing.com

....